JOHN HOOVER

ART & LIFE

JOHN HOOVER

Art & Life

BY JULIE DECKER

ANCHORAGE MUSEUM OF HISTORY AND ART
and
THE ANCHORAGE MUSEUM ASSOCIATION
in association with
UNIVERSITY OF WASHINGTON PRESS
Seattle and London

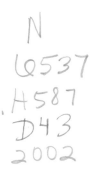
I would like to thank the following individuals for helping to make this project possible:
Judy Baletka, Georgia Blue, Don Decker, Michelle Decker, Don Ellegood,
John Hoover, Mary Hoover, John McKay, Don Mohr, J. T. Mohr, Michael Morris,
Dave Nicholls, Mary Randlett, Amy Tomson, Martha Vasikof, and Pat Wolf.

Library of Congress Cataloging-in-Publication Data

Decker, Julie, 1969-
   John Hoover : art & life / Julie Decker.
      p.cm.
   Includes bibliographicl references.
   ISBN 0-295-98177-6 (alk paper)
   1. Hoover, John, 1919-2. Indian artists--United States--Biography. I Title,

N6537.H587 D43 2002
709'.2--dc21

                                       2001046036

ISBN 0-295-98177-6 (cloth)
ISBN 0-295-98221-7 (paperback)

Printed in Hong Kong

Cover: *Shaman's Journey,* 2000
Back cover: *Puffin,* 1996

CONTENTS

☉ PREFACE

WHEN I FIRST MET ALEUT ARTIST JOHN HOOVER IN 1994, at an opening reception for an exhibition of his carvings, I was as charmed by John as I was by his work. Wise and mischievous, John lacks pretense, greeting friends with a bear hug rather than a handshake. It is impossible not to want to hear this man's stories. He is both warm and keenly intelligent. His life stories are not secrets but are intertwined with his artwork, and they are a gift to those who come to know him. It is my hope that this publication will bring John's stories and art to life for many more people and that it will preserve them for many more years.

I was introduced to Hoover's work while growing up in Alaska and visiting local museums and galleries. Like many Alaskans I experienced his artwork through the Municipality of Anchorage's public art program; Hoover created one of the most visible and significant public artworks in Anchorage, a collection of several life-sized sculptures depicting the Aleut legend of Volcano Woman. Encircling a seating area within Anchorage's William A. Egan Civic and Convention Center, the red cedar sculptures display Hoover's adept carving skills and his innovative approach to interpreting traditional Native American myths and legends. I immediately admired Hoover's work. It held a sophistication and grace that stretched beyond the boundaries of a specific culture or time. When I became the owner of a retail art gallery in Anchorage in 1994 and, with my father, plunged into the world of presenting and selling contemporary art to the public, exhibiting work like Hoover's was a standard to which we aspired.

The work on this publication began in 1999 as I was completing *Icebreakers: Alaska's Most Innovative Artists*, in which John was a featured artist. One day, while

WALRUS SPIRIT MASK, 1985
Cedar, 36 x 12 in.

working with John to acquire materials for *Icebreakers*, he jokingly suggested that the book should be just about him. I agreed that he was book-worthy. A week later, I called him again, this time saying that maybe a book about him was just what we should do. I bought a digital video camera and a tape recorder and went to visit John at his home and studio in Washington in late January 2000m while he was recuperating from triple-bypass heart surgery. I quizzed him about his life and his artwork, and he patiently told his stories.

John lives with his wife Mary and daughter Anna in a beautiful home on a quiet cove of Puget Sound in the small rural town of Grapeview. I felt privileged to visit them there and to be welcomed into their own private Eden. From the house a series of decks and stairs, hand-built by Hoover, leads through giant cedars, firs, and hemlocks to a sauna, guesthouse, and trail that takes Mary to a landing where she docks her kayak. John's studio is a mere ten feet from the home's front door.

The man who emerged in the interviews for this publication[1] has redefined the role of the artist. John demonstrated an ability to assess himself and his life in a perspective that he gained, not just with age, but also with having lived a life full of physical, mental, and aesthetic pleasures and challenges. Though he was tired and strained from his surgery, John still mesmerized me with his stories, wit, and thoughtful insight. The tales he spins are not just those told by the ancient Eskimos and Indians who inspired him—the stories are his own, revealing his zest for the out-of-ordinary experience and his quest for excellence. His stories are every bit as inspiring as the legends he re-creates.

John delivered boxes of articles and publications that had been written about him over the years, along with a stack of photographs, some dating back to 1900, which I sorted. I worked to compile the information into a complete biography and bibliography relating to John's life and art, and thank those photographers who provided documentation of Hoover's artwork as well as images of John himself throughout the years.

I am honored to have been chosen to write this publication and grateful for the new perspective on life that John's range of experiences and joy of life have revealed. Though he has now received much acclaim and his work is collected by museums throughout the world, he remains motivated primarily by his own need to create. With quiet dedication, he has lived the life of an artist for more than sixty years.

In the summer of 2000, I contacted Dave Nicholls, Exhibitions Curator at the Anchorage Museum of History and Art, and proposed that the museum serve as the host venue for a large retrospective exhibition of Hoover's work. Nicholls supported the idea and immediately set about to make it happen. It was important that the exhibition begin in Alaska, which was Hoover's home in his formative years, before it traveled throughout the United States to such cities as Seattle, Phoenix, and New York. The retrospective exhibition, like this publication, looks at John's entire art and life, from his upbringing in Cordova, Alaska, to his current life in Grapeview, Washington, from his early works in oil painting to his latest works in bronze. It is a tribute to Hoover and all that he has experienced and accomplished.

Although he left Alaska almost fifty years ago, Hoover's work will be forever tied to this state. John helped define both tradition and innovation and he redefined Alaska Native art. He is a craftsman, a skilled carver, and woodworker—a master. Because he combines these skills with a limitless imagination, he is also a creator.

JULIE DECKER
Decker / Morris Gallery

JOHN HOOVER
THE LIFE OF THE ARTIST

JOHN HOOVER'S QUEST FOR PERSONAL AND ARTISTIC INSPIRATION has been broad and tied not so much to his own Aleut and European heritage but drawn from the stories, myths, and legends of the many Native American cultures from throughout Alaska to the Northwest Coast and beyond. His interest in the Coast Salish people, for instance, is a predominant influence on his artwork and his choice of materials. The stories Hoover draws upon in creating his artwork have been passed down from generation to generation, over many centuries, and play a major role in the continuation of the culture. Hoover did not have elders to tell him these stories, so he discovered them through books.

Pan-Indian art is a term used to describe the art created by Native Americans that addresses Native themes, but that does not draw upon the traditions of any one particular tribe. Over the years, Native peoples borrowed ideas from neighboring tribes and from Europeans and other outsiders with whom they came into contact. The influences came about in a variety of ways. Some artists captured by other tribes and forced to work as slaves brought their own influences and traditions with them. In many areas, women married outside of their tribe, which also led to a mixing of traditions. Even before European contact, art objects were often traded between tribes across the continent. Although Pan-Indian art reflects the adaptability of Native peoples, it also, unfortunately, results from the destruction of the Native way of life, which has led to a loss of tribal identity. While Hoover draws on the stories, myths, and legends of many Native cultures, for him, Pan-Indian identity does not represent loss so much as celebration—celebration of the stories each culture has to offer and the respect each culture holds for its place and traditions.

If a story is not transmitted from one generation to the next, it will be irretrievably lost. The telling of stories is the way Native peoples maintained and con-

John Hoover at home in Grapevine, Washington, with his carvings, 1985.

tinued the creative process of the entire history and tradition of the culture, which is critical to survival. To some Native Americans, stories are revealed or entrusted to humans by spirit beings. Some stories are so powerful that if they can no longer be told accurately, they may become dangerous to humans. Individuals who know stories and who know how to perform rites are often considered powerful and wealthy, more so than someone who has compiled material goods.

Stories, however, are adaptable. Some stories have undergone extensive change from generation to generation, even from telling to telling. Many stories can be adapted and applied to many situations and are tools used to create and maintain community, identity, and family. Hoover has taken his responsibility for sharing ancient stories to heart. He has become a master storyteller, and his visual portrayals of ancient stories preserve them for many generations to come. He has adapted stories to make them his own and to make them relevant to his own time and place. He will smile when asked to tell a story represented in his artwork because the stories represent a joy of discovery and a connection to his past.

For indigenous peoples without a written language, art and oral traditions served as means of transmitting stories, history, and wisdom from generation to generation. Art, by depicting the history of the peoples, served as a constant reminder of the birthplaces of lineages and nations. Daily, mythological, and ceremonial life was intertwined with and expressed through art. Hoover feels he helps carry on this tradition.

Tlingit artist James Schoppert, a contemporary of Hoover's, expressed his view of Native arts in contemporary times:

> The exquisite work of our ancestors teaches us to create work suited for the day in which we live. By taking the old, breathing new life into it, and developing a new creation, the spirit of our people lives.

> We [Native artists] carry with us fragments of our culture and are now bringing those elements into the much broader scope of world civilization. We cannot return to the old ways, but we must retain the old ways and reflect them in our attitudes and in our art. This will be our contribution.[2]

The fragments of culture Hoover brings to his artwork are tales of shaman, spirit helpers, and the many creatures that were revered by the ancient cultures of Alaska and the Northwest. His artworks are about the transformation of humans into animal and animal into people, as spirits move from one world into another. They are about the sea, celebrating the birds, otters, walruses, and other creatures found along the northern coast. Hoover's own close relationship with nature is evidenced in his work—the creatures are powerful, beautiful, wise, and every bit as important as humans. Hoover is nostalgic for a way of life he never knew and a people he has only learned about through reading books and discovering ancient artifacts in museums. He has, nevertheless, developed a tremendous respect for the ancient way of life:

Fig. 1. *The artist's father, John Mervin Hoover, 1924, the year he died.*

Indians went to the college of life. They depended entirely upon their skills to sustain themselves; there were no Safeway stores to feed them. Their art was born of their feelings of self-preservation, working as a tribe— real values shared and handed down to future generations, through artwork, dances, storytelling and beliefs. Nature, of course, had a very important part in shaping their art. Their art was shaped by their real experiences with Mother Nature. I hope some of the work I have done portrays this ageless, spiritual wonderment, and brings solace and comfort to those who view them all with the same reverence I feel."[3]

It is important to Hoover to share his work with a diverse public—only in that way will he be able to preserve the ancient stories. He has exhibited, and others have collected, his artwork in Alaska and around the world. Hoover is grateful to the museums and galleries who took the initiative to exhibit contemporary Native work. He holds a special fondness for the Heard Museum in Phoenix, Arizona; the Philbrook Museum of Art in Tulsa, Oklahoma; the Anchorage Museum of History and Art, Alaska; the Institute of American Indian Arts, Santa Fe, New Mexico; as well as several art galleries in the Pacific Northwest, including the Stonington Gallery in Seattle and Anchorage; the Decker/Morris Gallery in Anchorage; Site 250 Fine Art Gallery and the Well Street Art Company in Fairbanks; the Haines Gallery in Everett and Seattle; the Daybreak Star Center in Seattle and their Sacred Circle galleries; and the Quintana Gallery in Portland, Oregon. The Glen Green Galleries in Santa Fe and Scottsdale, Arizona, have also been instrumental in making Hoover's work available to the public and to prominent collectors.

Hoover's work has evolved from paintings to simple carvings to complex cutouts featuring symmetrical and asymmetrical forms that fold and unfold into diptychs and triptychs, transforming as the ancient spirit helpers transformed in the stories Hoover works to retell. Hoover has dedicated his life to creating artwork and learning about Native cultures. In getting to know Hoover and his work, one can't help but develop respect for the people and traditions of the Pacific Northwest and Alaska.

Fig. 2. *From left to right: Jake Hoover, Annie Hoover, Violet Hoover (John's father, mother and sister), Katalla, Alaska, 1905.*

BEGINNINGS

John Jay Hoover was born on October 13, 1919, in Cordova, Alaska. Hoover's father, Jay Mervin Hoover (known as "Jake"), was born in 1862 to a family of Dutch ancestry (fig. 1). Jake was an accomplished musician who earned his living in Montana as a hunter for the railroad. Jake was also a prospector, and when he discovered an emerald mine and sold it for a handsome profit, he followed his dream to move to Alaska—a place where many went to seek their fortune.

In this rugged land, Jake Hoover met Annie Serakovikoff. Annie was of Aleut descent, born in 1873 in Unga, one of the Shumagin Islands southwest of the Alaska Peninsula. Alaska Natives are not a homogeneous group and are broadly separated into Aleuts, Eskimos, and Indians, belonging to more than twenty language and culture groups. Within those groups, Alaska Natives have particular village and tribal affiliations and each group identifies a different geographic region where their ancient ancestors lived.

The Russians were the first newcomers of the modern era, drawn to Alaska in the mid-1700s in pursuit of sea otters and their valuable pelts. The Aleut suffered the most from Russian contact, first subjugated, then decimated by disease, and ultimately inculcated into Russian culture through the efforts of Russian Orthodox missionaries. The Russians quickly depleted the sea otter population in the Aleutian Islands, on which the Aleut depended for food, and soon moved eastward for more pelts. The Russian legacy throughout Alaska included smallpox and venereal disease, both of which wreaked havoc on Native populations.

The Russian presence in the Aleutian Islands was still dominant when Annie Serakovikoff was growing up. Annie's father died when she was a child, and she was sent to an orphanage in Unalaska run by Russian priests, who loaned her to a family to do menial tasks. At the age of seventeen, she heard that her mother was on Kodiak Island and sick with tuberculosis. She went to Kodiak to care for her,

Fig. 3. *David and Annie Kozachuk, 1960 (John's mother and stepfather).*

Fig. 4. *Elenore Hoover, (John's sister), 1927.*

but her mother died later that same year. Instead of returning to Unalaska, Annie fled to Katalla, Alaska, where she met Jake.

Jake and Annie Hoover lived at Yakataga Beach, near Katalla, for several years where they mined for gold (fig. 2). Jake also worked as a fisherman. In 1919 the couple moved to Cordova so that Annie could give birth to son John, their third child, in a Cordova hospital. John Hoover was the youngest of Jake and Annie's three children. He had an older sister, Violet, and a younger sister, Elenore (fig. 4). Shortly after John's birth, they moved back to Katalla.

In 1924, when John was five years old, Jake and Annie returned to Cordova, but shortly after the move, Jake died of appendicitis while working on a mail boat in the Gulf of Alaska. Annie supported the family by working in fisheries, mining camps, laundries, and as a cook in oil fields, often preparing meals for more than eighty men. Annie could tan all types of animal skins and was an accomplished taxidermist as well as a talented musician. Annie lived in a tiny home (fig. 7) in Cordova until her death at age eighty-seven. It had been partially built and repaired by Jake with scraps left over from the construction of Cordova's noted Windsor Hotel.

The city of Cordova, where the Hoover children were raised, was not a place concerned with tradition. It was a boom town, with new wealth and a diverse mix of people and industries. Located on Prince William Sound in the Gulf of Alaska, southeast of Anchorage, Cordova is today a small fishing town, but it was once the terminus of the Copper River and Northwestern Railroad, which carried copper ore two hundred miles from the Kennecott mine in the Chitina Valley to the ocean. The building of the mine brought two or three thousand people to Cordova, making it Alaska's largest city during Hoover's childhood (fig. 5,6).

While the railroad and mining provided work for many residents, many others found work fishing, including Native Alaskans, particularly the Eyak Indians—

Fig. 5. *Cordova from Mt. Eyak, 1930. Photograph courtesy of the Anchorage Museum of History and Art.*

the earliest people to settle in the Cordova area. By the 1880s, several canneries had opened in the region to take advantage of the gulf's abundant salmon. Cordova flourished as docks and tramways were built on Eyak Lake to transport the fish. Fishing had also provided work for both Jake and Annie Hoover, with Jake working the boats while Annie worked in canneries.

Hoover's memories of Cordova include restaurants, bars, roller rinks, tennis courts, and philharmonic orchestras. He remembers it was "like living in New York, only smaller." Although Cordova had a Bureau of Indian Affairs school (a government-sponsored school, like many others set up in remote territories, as part of an effort to assimilate indigenous populations), Hoover was educated at public schools, and he also attended the Presbyterian Church and music lessons. The Hoover family was quite musical: Elenore, the youngest girl, played the violin, Jake and Annie played the fiddle and harmonica—at home and at dances. Violet, the eldest, sang ballads and played the guitar. Hoover himself played the piano by ear and wrote music and lyrics.

Hoover says the only thing that got him through school was mathematics. He excelled in math, but he also enjoyed art, taking classes in drawing, sketching, and composition. In grade school, Hoover frequently won American Legion poster contests, held every spring in Cordova. During these elementary years Hoover first experimented with oil paintings, imitating his sister Violet, a talented artist who excelled at sketching. "I thought it was a form of magic," recalled Hoover.[4]

Outside school, Hoover recalls bird watching along the Copper River, still famous today for its wide range of species. Hunting also was a hobby, as were skiing and skating. Most activities centered on Eyak Lake, the focal point of the town. Natural gas from the lake created large gas "pockets," some of them five and six feet in diameter. Hoover and his friends would skate along the lake on winter nights and

Fig. 6. Downtown Cordova, Alaska, 1930. Photograph courtesy of the Anchorage Museum of History and Art.

poke holes in the pockets with small nails. They would light the gas, and watch the pockets burn all night long.

While seemingly a normal and blissful early childhood, Hoover's early years were not without challenges and tension. Hoover's mother kept John's hair long when he was young—a custom that had been developed more than one hundred years before to disguise Aleut boys as girls so they would not be conscripted for hunting by the Russian fur traders; Hoover did not have his hair cut until he was five years old (fig. 8). He recounts the ancient threat of the Russian fur traders in this way:

> Russian fur traders, during the eighteenth and nineteenth centuries, killed many Aleut people in their greed for the quick profit they could reap from selling the sea otter pelts to Chinese lords. During the period, mothers of boys disguised their sons as girls to save them from conscription, from "Hunters of the Sea Otter Death Syndrome."

His Aleut heritage made him an outsider at times, despite his mother's efforts and the diverse population of Cordova:

> I was raised in an urban setting in the territory of Alaska, under martial law. Indians were ordered by the federal government to be assimilated. English was the only language allowed in the schools. Bigotry and prejudice were prevalent. My father was called "squaw man." Cordova was the hub of activity created by the railroad serving the copper mines. It was a bonanza for everyone. Every nationality was represented there with their own culture—foods, restaurants, lifestyles—everyone was welcome there but the Indian. My Aleut mother, in a desperate attempt to make us acceptable, raised us as white. The town had an Indian School but somehow she kept us in the public school. There were some that questioned our presence, but eventually we were accepted.[5]

From the ages of seven to fourteen, Hoover earned wages as a boxer at monthly

Fig. 7. *The Hoover home, Cordova, Alaska, 1927.*

fights in Cordova. He also fought outside the ring in local youth gang wars:

> While my sister attended orchestra rehearsals, I expressed myself by taking part in gang wars. These weren't really racial conflicts, although there was plenty of animosity toward non-whites and that increased the tension. As a U.S. territory under federal law, federal marshals administered Alaska. They were power moguls who intimidated the Natives, invaded their homes, and pillaged their art until there was nothing left of the culture.[6]

By the age of fifteen, Hoover was earning money fishing and by the age of twenty-one, he had switched from smoker fights to playing drums in Cordova bars.

Art ultimately led Hoover back to his Aleut heritage, but his development as an artist began slowly. Many painters visited Cordova in the 1920s and 30s, including such well-known artists of the Pacific Northwest as Sydney Laurence, Ted Lambert, Jules Dahlager, and Eustace Ziegler. Those who were not permanent residents of Alaska often came north to paint the grand Alaskan landscape and would gather in the evening to paint in the lobby of Cordova's grand Windsor Hotel. They are still some of Alaska's most beloved and collected historical painters. "It was magic watching them," said Hoover, "They had their easels set up there...so that probably had an influence on me, watching them paint like that." Hoover never spoke to the visiting artists but their presence made an impression on him. He particularly remembers seeing them seated before the enormous fireplace in the hotel with their canvases of mountain scenery and seascapes. Hoover also remembers admiring the work of Josephine Crumbine, an Alaska artist who made frequent trips to Cordova in the 1930s and 1940s. Crumbine specialized in paintings of animals and is best known for a set of menu illustrations of sled dogs that she created in the 1950s for the Alaska Steamship Company.

Hoover took an extra year to finish high school, because he chose to dig clams

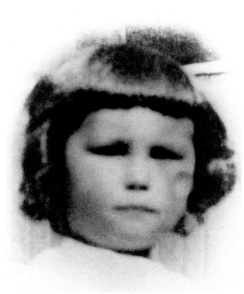

Fig. 8. *John Hoover,*
age 4, 1923.

Fig. 9. *John Hoover,*
age 8, 1927.

rather than attend classes most springs. He was one of the best clam diggers in the area, collecting one thousand pounds of clams in one tide and averaging seventy-five dollars a day. Hoover also worked for fifteen cents an hour in the salmon canneries and for forty cents an hour on the railroad in a tie-tamping camp. Following graduation from Cordova High School in 1938, he worked at many odd jobs, including as a pile driver, shipwright (carpenter), and machinist's helper. He even had his own taxicab stand. Fishing, however, was the most consistent activity in Hoover's life, and he even built his own boats.

While earning a living at these odd jobs, Hoover also continued to experiment with oil painting, although he claims never to have sold a single completed work. "I couldn't sell the damn things. Fifty to seventy-five dollars a painting—big paintings—and it was impossible. There were too many other painters around." Although most of his paintings depicted images of fishing boats and the sea, Hoover did tackle many other themes and styles. "When I was painting, I got into everything: Cubism, Impressionism, I tried them all. I had several books on different artists," said Hoover. He learned his techniques by reviewing how-to art books by Walter Foster. Using these books, Hoover experimented with painting, drawing, and working in perspective, mostly creating images of fishing boats and stormy seas. The income from commercial fishing allowed Hoover to paint for the eight to nine months of each year that he wasn't at sea. "I just did what I wanted to do. What I felt was pleasing to me, you know, rewarding," said Hoover.

Cordova was the site of a major military buildup during World War II. Although many Cordovans joined the military, fishing was considered important to the war effort, and good fishermen were given deferments to continue their trade.

"I was a draft dodger for two years," laughs Hoover, who eventually was drafted

Fig. 10. *Annie Hoover (right) and friend Pearl Hodnut, Cordova, Alaska, 1920.*

Fig. 11. *Aleuts on board ship at Unalaska, being relocated away from the war zone during the summer of 1942.*

when he was twenty-three and served in the U.S. Army Transportation Service, skippering an eighty-five-foot power barge based at Unalaska that supplied military posts throughout the stormy Aleutians. By war's end, he was a master sergeant, commanding a 138-foot freight and passenger ship on assignment in Alaska, which won him a Navy Citation for salvage work (figs. 12–15).

> I was fishing and had a deferment, but they finally caught up with me. I was working for [the construction company] Morrison Knudson who had a deferment in the winter, but I finally got drafted. And a week after I got drafted, we were supposed to go to the South Pacific—with an engineering company. We went to Whittier [Alaska] and worked on clearing land for an army post for a week, and then I got lucky. Howard Wakefield, who was in charge of the harbor-craft detachment, had about thirty boats and nobody to run them; and he just didn't know what the hell to do, so he got me out of the engineers, and a month after I was in the Army I was back home running a boat. I was really lucky, except I had to go to the Aleutian Islands for three years, and that was really tough. A lot of people drowned there—not from warfare, just the weather. I've been sort of lucky all my life. That was real lucky because the guys that went, some got shot up and killed.

Like many servicemen discharged from the Army, Hoover used the G.I. Bill for training. He took an unusual approach, traveling to Seattle for two months of Fred Astaire dance lessons as well as piano lessons. Upon returning to Cordova, Hoover again turned to the sea, purchasing a power barge called the *Red Head*:

> We went all over, hauling lumber and fuel, towing logs, and brailing salmon. Used to go out to Seattle every winter. We had that barge for about three years, and then we sold it. Paid eight thousand dollars for it; it was only three months old. Eighty-

Fig. 12. *John Hoover, age 18, 1937.*

Fig. 13. *Sargeant John Hoover, Skipper, 1943.*

five-foot-long barge. We used it for three years and sold it for fifty thousand dollars. Got lucky, I guess.

After the war, Hoover worked not only at painting and fishing, but also as a drummer in a dance band in Cordova three nights a week. He had learned to play the drum with the American Legion drum and bugle corps during the war, and he traveled with them from city to city, where contests were held. Hoover was the Sergeant Drummer. "With stripes, you know," he said with a smile.

In 1946 Hoover married Barbara McAllister, a Montana-born twenty-year-old who was living in Palmer, Alaska, when she met Hoover. In the years following the marriage, Hoover continued working as a commercial fisherman and shipwright to support his growing family. Barbara and John would eventually have five children, all named after Catholic saints: Mark, born 1949; Martha, born 1950; Tony, born 1951; Grace Ann, born 1955; and Jane, born 1964.

In 1950 Hoover was determined to become a serious painter. He ordered a small oil painting set from the Sears-Roebuck catalog: "There was one piece of board and I cut it up into four pieces, each just four by six inches. There was one little brush." He completed four works. *Cannery Row* (plate 1) features a waterfront scene and the long row of canneries that lined the shore. "Turned out pretty good, really," declared Hoover, who is still in possession of these early attempts. *Mt. Eccles, Cordova, Alaska* (plate 2) celebrated the mountains that surround Cordova. "Everyone in Alaska had painted this one [Mt. Eccles]—like Mount McKinley, almost," he laughed. *Lake Eyak, Cordova, Alaska* (plate 3) was a depiction of Eyak Lake and the road from the town that leads to the lake. The fourth small board was used to create a pencil sketch called *Fishing Grounds*. In 2001, Hoover still considered *Mt. Eccles, Cordova, Alaska* one of his best paintings.

LIFE AS A PAINTER

In 1952 Hoover and his young family left Cordova and moved to Edmonds, Washington. The move was prompted by an invitation from the Anchorage Ski Club to take fifty skiers to Sun Valley on a DC3 cargo airplane. Hoover was one of three from an Alaska racing team that went along. They were able to ski with Ziggy Engle, a Scandinavian Olympic skier who was chosen to run the ski school in Sun Valley when it first opened. Hoover entertained dreams of being a ski instructor in Sun Valley, after a personal invitation to do so from Engle, but after the initial trip, he never returned to Idaho.

In Edmonds, Hoover continued to pursue his interest in art, becoming a member of Seattle Co-Arts, joining thirty-five women and one other man—all painters. The group shared a co-op gallery in Bellevue and would go on painting excursions around the Seattle area, most often to the waterfront.

Many members of Seattle Co-Arts had previously attended the Leon Derbyshire School of Fine Art. The school specialized in drawing and painting and occupied the entire fourteenth floor of a Seattle high-rise. Hoover, too, attended Leon Derbyshire for three years, from 1957 to 1960, studying with Derbyshire himself. "I think you have to have a background like that," said Hoover. "You have to have some lessons. You have to have a good teacher." Hoover credits Derbyshire with truly teaching him how to paint, offering instruction in both techniques and style. Hoover also remembers brief interactions with other Seattle-area painters, such as Guy Anderson, Morris Graves, and Mark Tobey, who would later become artists with international reputations. He says being in the continual presence of other artists helped him to stay dedicated to developing his own artwork.

The paintings Hoover created during this time, in the late 1950s and early 1960s, varied in both theme and style. Most were reminiscences of his years in Cordova, although others did reflect his current life and setting. *Eyak Church,* 1959

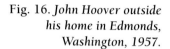

< Fig. 14. *Crew of the P.B. 109, U.S. Army, 1945. John Hoover is at upper left.*

Fig. 15. *John Hoover aboard* Red Head, *a surplus power barge, 1945.*

Fig. 16. *John Hoover outside his home in Edmonds, Washington, 1957.*

Fig. 17. *The Aldebaran, built by Hoover.*

(plate 7), depicts a Russian Orthodox Church in Cordova. Hoover recalls Russian Orthodox celebrations, in which the Eyak Indians of Cordova took part.

> We lived uptown. Downtown—old town—was where the Eyaks lived. During certain Russian Orthodox holidays they would build prayer wheels and would walk with the wheels to the homes of townspeople they knew that were part Indian or Aleut. People would give them food. I just vaguely remember it. I made this painting of what I thought it looked like.

Other Alaska-inspired paintings feature fishing. *Putting Out the Lead*, 1960 (plate 9), and *Stake Net*, 1961 (plate 10), depict rough Alaskan seas and mountains. *Stake Net* is a tribute to Hoover's father, who fished in both Katalla and Cordova. The stake nets were gill nets set on poles, forming a trap—something that is no longer permitted in Alaskan waters. "I started fishing in 1928 and have continued to fish my whole life, more than seventy years," said Hoover. "Fishing was one of the reasons why I could be an artist—I didn't have to depend on the money from selling art." Hoover both reveres and fears the sea. It is a relationship to nature that Hoover wishes to share:

> Like all fathers, I wish to pass on to my sons a means of livelihood, and as much as is possible, an understanding of life itself. The sea and fishing are great teachers of patience, respect, close harmony with other men, tolerance, a highly competitive spirit of camaraderie, a nearness to God and ready access to the bountiful bosom of His Mother Nature.[7]

Fish Camp, 1959 (plate 8), depicts a fishing scene closer to Hoover's life in Edmonds. Hoover used to visit the Tulalip Indian reservation, particularly in the late 1950s when he was sketching a lot of the time. On the reservation he encountered a fish camp where the Tulalips kept their fishing boats and gear. Hoover watched them set nets using just skiffs and outboards for fishing boats. The scene made Hoover homesick for Cordova

Fig. 18. *John Hoover, Rialto Beach, Washington, 1976.*

Fig. 19. *John and Barbara Hoover on a beach in Edmonds, Washington, 1971.*

and he sketched the scene on site, later working it into a fully developed painting.

Other paintings were more obviously personal to the artist. *Self-portrait,* 1957 (plate 6), is dominated by a back view of the artist staring out over a tulip field on the Tulalip reservation. *Out My Studio Window,* 1956 (plate 4), is a view from the largest plate glass window of the two-story studio Hoover had built adjacent to his Edmonds home (fig. 16). The title of the painting and the construction of the studio demonstrate Hoover's willingness to identify himself as an artist, something he had been reluctant to do prior to moving to Edmonds. Hoover's daughter Martha recalls the Hoovers' Edmonds' home as a brown ranch-style house with beautiful views of Puget Sound. Martha remembers Hoover's studio smelling of cedar, linseed oil, and turpentine. Jazz music, particularly by Miles Davis, was always playing "really loud" as Hoover worked. She said it was a fun place to explore, but clearly "Dad's domain."

The 1950s were consumed by fatherhood for Hoover, with three children born that decade. Hoover's children recall a father who led by example rather than words and who stressed individuality and a thoughtful approach to life. Hoover represented a different kind of spirituality to his children from that of their mother Barbara, who was Catholic. Hoover did not go to church with the family. "The spirits of the sea and the forest were what Dad worshipped," explained Martha.

> And he worships the Creator that made all of that—the source of all things. This wasn't anything spoken. We just knew. Just watching how a person salts fish, steers a boat or works with wood. That's how you can feel someone's spirituality—that's how Dad showed his spirituality. It was just innate. There weren't any lesson books.

The children learned of their Aleut heritage by observing their father, rather than by anything he told them directly. Each child would ultimately go back to

Alaska in adulthood to discover his or her own heritage. Martha credits her father with her desire to reclaim her heritage:

> My love for my ancestry is from my father. With my green eyes, dark hair, and high cheekbones, I don't necessarily look Native. But ever since I reached adulthood, I've been in politics, involved in efforts to revive Native culture in villages, and involved in programs throughout Alaska to promote pride and cultural values. I attribute that to the love I have for my grandmother and something I picked up from my dad—the pride he has in his Native heritage in spite of all the prejudice he experienced growing up.

Hoover also instilled a deep respect for art and artistic traditions in his children. Martha recalls that following their artistic impulses was strongly encouraged:

> What he did get through to me loud and clear was family values and what is expected of you in a family sense. What was expected of us was to be one of a kind. There always seemed to be a test of creativity. Creativity was what was valued more than materialism or anything else. There was even a push for all of us to study the violin because that was Elenore's instrument. Grace Ann could play the violin. I couldn't; but we're all artistic in our own way. Every part of our being either had something to do with art or fish.

Martha remembers their family being "different" from other families: "When we went on family outings, we'd go to museums and galleries and spend all day there. We'd spread out and each go where we wanted to go and see what we wanted to see." The Hoovers often visited the Seattle Art Museum. They would also go on outings to visit other local artists or travel to Neah Bay to visit the Makah reservation. "We'd load up the station wagon and head to Neah Bay and stay with friends who had a hotel," remembers Martha. "People from the reservation taught us how to eat gooseneck barnacles and things from off the reef."

The Hoovers would live in Edmonds in the winter months and travel each spring to Cordova, where they kept a family boat. For the first few years, Hoover would travel back to Alaska alone, spending the summer away from the family, which stayed in Edmonds. But by 1964, after youngest daughter Jane was born, the whole family would fish for salmon and gill net together in Prince William Sound. They would also visit Annie, Hoover's mother, while in Alaska. Commercial fishing in the summer supplied the family with enough income to live on the remainder of the year and allowed Hoover to work on his art full-time in the winter months.

In the late 1950s, in addition to exhibiting at the Co-Arts gallery in Bellevue, Hoover was showing his work at the Haines Gallery in Seattle and had a small exhibition at the Capitol Museum in Olympia, Washington. In 1960 Hoover finally sold one of his paintings: the Seattle Art Museum purchased *The Gleaners*, 1958, for its permanent collection. Dr. Richard E. Fuller, founder of the Seattle Art Museum, was a friend of John and Barbara Hoover's, often dining with them socially. In 1960 Fuller invited Hoover to the museum to show him his paintings. He asked Hoover how much he wanted for them. "Fifty bucks," replied Hoover. Fuller selected *The Gleaners* and made the purchase for the museum himself. The painting was a depiction of Seattle's homeless, whom Hoover often observed when he picked up his wife Barbara in the alley behind a hotel restaurant where she worked. Hoover recalled that each "gleaner" had his own garbage can staked out; most had many pockets

Fig. 20. *Inside the Hoover home in Edmonds, 1971.*

Fig. 21. *One of John Hoover's first major exhibitions at the Whatcom Museum, Bellingham, Washington, 1971.*

sewn into their clothing or overcoats where they placed food scraps. Hoover visited the alley one day specifically to sketch them, and later created a painting based on his sketch. Hoover was quite pleased that the Seattle Art Museum valued his work enough to purchase one of his paintings, but his own interest soon thereafter turned from painting to sculpture.

EARLY CARVINGS

Hoover and an Edmonds neighbor had worked together in 1958 in Hoover's backyard to build a fifty-eight-foot Alaskan limit-seiner out of wood. Modeled after the fishing boats commonly used in the Northwest and Alaska, the boat was made almost entirely of old growth fir, with white oak from Tennessee making up the ribs. Hoover had learned to build boats from a shipwright, a master craftsman, in Cordova.

Hoover and his neighbor lacked the proper power tools for building the boat, however, and had to shape the timbers by hand. The boat, the *Aldebaran*—named after one of the brightest stars in the northern hemisphere—is still working today out of Port Townsend, Washington (fig. 17). Building the *Aldebaran* made Hoover see possibilities for applying his woodworking skills to art. He began to think about trading his brushes for a chisel. "It's natural for a painter to turn into a sculptor," said Hoover. "A lot of people paint first. It's just a natural progression, I guess. I don't know whether you have to be able to paint first to be a sculptor or not, but probably."

Hoover's daughter Martha remembers that while her father was working on the *Aldebaran*, he would find small scraps of wood with wormholes in them. He would cut the wood into different shapes, not carving them, but cutting out rough figures and fish shapes. He would then hang them, like mobiles, from the ceiling of his studio—a hint of his later interest in creating large-scale sculptures that hung in space. Martha also recalls that wooden floats made by Hoover decorated the fence that enclosed their yard. She theorized that Hoover made these to let everyone know

Fig. 22. *John Hoover (second from left), artist-in-residence through Air Force school system, Manila, Phillipines, 1974.*

Fig. 23. *Mobile/installation at King County Courthouse, 1978.*

a fisherman lived there. He also practiced his woodworking skills by making traditional Aleut hunting hats, but rather than use the bentwood method typical of most Native craftsmen, Hoover would carve his out of one piece of wood.

Martha sees a strong connection between her father's carvings and the traditional masks made in ancient times in the Aleut village of Unga. "When I see those masks, I can see Dad's work," she mused. "It's not anything studied. He has an ancestral knowledge of Aleut art; an innate sense of ancient geometric shapes and motifs that comes somewhere from within. I think he descends from ancestor carvers." Although Hoover was not interested in replicating Aleut masks, he was looking for ways to combine traditional themes with his new interest in wood, hoping to find a style of his own.

When Hoover first started using wood to create sculptures, his works were oil-painted designs on cedar planks, inspired by traditional Aleut spirit boards, hinged decorated panels featuring an image representing a family, clan, lineage, or a high-ranking individual that serves as a prop during ceremonial performances. The figures in Hoover's works represented spirits, with simplified body forms and stick-like arms and hands. His color use in these early works is minimal, with a white wash used to create the bodies of the figures.

Around 1960 Hoover started carving into the wood rather than just painting on it. He would begin his carvings with a pencil sketch on scratch paper, which he would then transfer to brown butcher paper (fig. 27). He rubbed the paper over the actual piece of wood he intended to carve to get a sense of the contours of the wood. He then rubbed charcoal over the paper to further delineate the contours. Next Hoover refined his imprint with carbon paper and traced it back onto a piece of wood, like a template. "You just can't start carving a piece of wood unless you know what the heck you're doing," says Hoover. Ancient Alaskan and Northwest carving (bentwood boxes, utilitarian

Fig. 24. *John Hoover's home and studio in Grapeview, Washington, 1978.*

and other objects) also involved the use of templates like those Hoover had devised, but he modified the tradition. The designs used in his templates are his own, not ancient patterns.

These early, fully realized carvings were also Hoover's version of spirit boards. The form was inspired by a collection of ancient Coast Salish spirit boards at the Washington State Museum in Tacoma whose simplicity Hoover admired (plate 16). His own spirit boards were produced in a Northwest style but with his personal interpretations of the Coast Salish and Tlingit and Haida Indian myths that inspired them:

> When I first started carving, I did as many do: by imitating the Northwest Coast carvers of Washington and Canada. I picked the Salish style, not the regulated approach dictated by so-called experts who were and still are dictating what is Indian Art. You don't have to be Indian to create Indian Art; all you have to do is be able to learn how to carve and then "follow the rules." Salish art is different. There were no rules. It was crude but powerful spiritually. It was important to the people. Imagine the whale hunters getting into a log dugout canoe and going searching for a whale! You had to believe in yourself to do this![8]

Unlike his later pieces, Hoover did not carve on both sides of these panels. *Phoenix Bird*, 1968 (plate 13), is a simplified frontal view of the Phoenix as it rises out of a flame (Native legends have the Phoenix rising every two hundred years). Here, Hoover has created a louvered effect for the background, carving layered stripes into the wood. The wings of the Phoenix are also layered to create the illusion of feathers. At the tips of the bird's wings are two human faces, representing the spirit helpers.

Almost all of Hoover's work incorporates some representation of the human form. The faces almost always hold the same serene expression. They are inspired by "Madonna" figurines of the Okvik period, dating back approximately two thousand years. The small

Fig. 25. *John Hoover at home in Grapeview, Washington, with his* Ancestor Figures *before they were installed at the Daybreak Star Center in Seattle, Washington, 1977.*

walrus ivory figures have been found scattered throughout Alaska and are considered the oldest remnants of the Northern maritime culture. They represent the spirit, or *inua,* which means "owner" or "indweller" to many North American peoples. *Inua* is the all-pervasive spirit with whom the shamans were able to communicate. Every object has its *inua*—even air possesses one. The human *inua* is the soul.[9]

The faces and figures in Hoover's work are also symbolic of Native ancestors, which are very important in all Alaska Native and Northwest Coast cultures. In Northwest Coast art, a human portrait often represents an ancestor figure, who is no less real for being mythical. Full human figures may also be guardians—protective talismans—or personifications of such environmental phenomena as the sun. In most Northwest Coast art, when smaller animal figures are carved in relief on the cheeks or foreheads of human faces, the figures represent spirit helpers. They signify the shaman's gifts and skills, which include powers of transformation and access to sacred knowledge.

Hoover gathered much of his information about ancient cultures from books. "I was never lucky enough to experience any real traditional material. I had to read about it. Luckily, I was able to take traditional material and make it into my own vision. I am thankful for that gift." One of the books Hoover remembers listed three thousand Indian tribes of the United States from "A" to "Z" and described each of them; others described some of the myths and legends of the Aleut peoples. During the late 1960s and 1970s a friend who was a book dealer interested Hoover in ethnology books from the Smithsonian Institution, in which he found some classic illustrations of early Northwest Coast art.[10] These books acquainted Hoover with his own heritage and with other Native cultures. They featured masks, descriptions of materials used in making ceremonial objects, tools for hunting and fishing, traditional decorations found on utilitarian and ceremonial objects, and folklore and mythology. The books influenced Hoover more than any artist or art movement. It

Fig. 26. *Inside John* >
Hoover's Grapeview,
Washington, studio, 1976.

Fig. 27. *Sketches*
and templates used by
John Hoover in creating
his artwork.

was through reading these books that Hoover discovered the narratives he wanted to tell visually. It was the books that gave him an appreciation for what had been lost and what could still be preserved and Hoover sought other books about the Aleuts and the peoples of the Northwest Coast.

One of Hoover's most beloved books is *Shamanism: The Beginnings of Art.* Written in 1967 by Andreas Lommel, the director of the National Museum of Ethnology in Munich, the book describes shamans as the first psychologists, doctors, and artists. Of shamans, Lommel writes:

> Unlike the medicine man, the future shaman acts under an inner compulsion...a psychosis that is emerging for some reason or other [and] is so strong that the only way out open to the individual attacked by it is to escape from its shamanistic activity, that is to say, essentially by means of artistic productivity, such as dancing or singing, which always involves a state of trance.[11]

Hoover is interested in the shaman more than any other figure in Native American culture and history. He has also studied the role of the shaman in a community, the powers of the shaman, and the shaman's relationship with spirit helpers:

> For the shaman, pieces of wood, rocks, and stones are alive and possess energy. A rock has a body, a log has grain. Shamans are the original psychologists. They draw out images from the subconscious. They bring what is fearful out into the open, so that people can cope with it.[12]

Many North American Indian myths concern the powers of shamans. While in some cases the shaman inherits his or her role, it is more common for them to be summoned by the spirits, usually against their will. The spirits drive them out into isolation until they achieve enlightenment. When he or she then accepts this vocation, all the secrets of the universe are revealed and a relationship with spiritual aids and guides can begin.

Shamans can be vehicles for transformation, which is one of the overarching themes in Hoover's work. Although he never found a book specifically addressing the shamanic powers of transformation in Aleut culture, Hoover believes transformation is a concept that spans all religions and that it is what draws others to his artwork:

> The transformation mythology, that's one of my main themes, and people relate to that; they find somehow a religious connotation to it, a spiritual adventure, which is good, but I don't do that on purpose. It seems to come out in my work. Although I can't myself transform into any other shape, I can through my art. And transformation has become very important in my art.

Communities practicing shamanism believe that most illnesses are the result of a loss of one's soul. The shaman cures the person by retrieving his or her soul. Shamans have spirit helpers who assist them in their search for a sick person's soul—if the soul is not found the patient will die. A spirit helper can change into a loon underwater, or into a bird that can fly, or a forest animal, to find the soul and return it to be put back into the patient. "I have become associated with birds in my art. Birds were, and still are, very important to me with their ability to transform into spirit helpers," said Hoover.[13] Hoover's artwork is often a representation of these spirit helpers, and many of the titles to his work include the word "spirit" such as *Wolf Spirit* and *Owl Spirit.*

MATERIALS AND METHODS

Hoover took care to select the best tools and materials. He bought lumber in hardware stores, including cedar and mahogany. Cedar soon became his wood of choice. The cedar Hoover uses in his carvings is almost one thousand years old and comes from the forests of western Washington, where it flourishes along the rainforest coast of the Pacific Northwest with spruce, Douglas fir, hemlock, and other conifers.

All marine-oriented peoples of the Northwest Coast who lived in or near the great evergreen forests consider cedar supernatural and have held the wood in the highest esteem. They used the wood to build houses and boats, while the bark was used to weave baskets, mats, clothing, curtains, and spiritual objects.

Great cedar trees with a true, clear grain are becoming more and more difficult to find along the Northwest Coast, due to logging, the pressure of burgeoning populations, and urban expansion. Many contemporary Native people are working to reclaim their traditional art forms, and the cedar tree is central to that art, providing raw material in the form of wood, bark, roots, and twigs. Women are reviving traditional weaving skills and making baskets, and men are carving crest poles, canoes, steambent boxes, masks, drums, and rattles. Even large plank houses, traditional community structures, are again being built and used for feasts and ceremonies. Yet the tree that was plentiful hundreds and thousands of years ago for these uses is no longer abundant.

Hoover is especially fond of the red cedar, found at elevations from sea level to four or five thousand feet, and ranging from Baranof Island in Alaska southward down the coast of British Columbia through Washington and Oregon to northern California. The finest cedars are not found along the coast, but are rooted in the deeper, moister, more porous soils of lakesides, estuaries, cool slopes, and rich bottom lands.[14] In the shade of dense forests, cedars reach up for light, and the resulting tall, straight

Fig. 28a–f. *John Hoover at work in his Grapeview, Washington, studio, 1976.*

trunk is uninterrupted by branches for much of its height—a characteristic prized for monumental sculpture.

Beneath the red cedar's pale sapwood is straight-grained heartwood in shades of reddish brown that has a characteristic scent. Red cedar has better insulating properties than hardwoods, but it is not as strong. Air spaces and cleavage planes inherent in the cedar make this both a very light wood and allow it to be readily split, important traits for Native Northwest Coast builders. Cedar is a very soft wood for carving, making the final sculptures quite soft and fragile as well.

For many generations, the cedar tree was valued because it could be worked in so many ways with a minimum of tools. Woodworking skills were refined over time, and the simplicity of the tools employed is a testament to the skills, knowledge, and experience of Northwest carvers. A major woodworking industry developed along the entire Northwest Coast wherever cedar grew. Today, a revival of woodworking flourishes along the Northwest Coast, and several top artists are taking on apprentices to pass on the craft.

Woodworking was solely the task of men in ancient Northwest cultures. Men constructed containers for fishing and hunting gear, tools, household implements, dugout canoes, houses, and many other things. Men's carving tools were very personal items, each tool made to fit the worker's individual hands and ways of working. Sometimes, a specific tool was devised for a particular need. These were treasured items, and a woodworker often sculptured the handles of his tools with intricate crest figures. The hammer, wedge, and adze were the three basic tools, while a number of other specialized tools were used for specific techniques or tasks.

Because Hoover never lived within an Aleut community, he did not have master Aleut carvers to teach him their ancient craft and was largely self-taught in the techniques of woodcarving. He did find some books that showed how to make and

use carving knives, methods that were used long ago. While working as an artist-in-residence in Japan and the Pacific Islands, Hoover learned some ancient Eastern carving strategies, which he also adapted to suit his own craft and style. Hoover says the tools he has used over the decades have become sacred objects to him (figs. 29-31). One, which he believes is prehistoric, is a large, smooth rock that he uses to put the characteristic indentations into his work.

Even when using the ancient Eskimo tools to finish the finer aspects of his carving, Hoover has modified them, changing each as necessary to fit a particular project. He also uses power tools, including a band saw, sanders, and other aids. "You have to adapt," said Hoover. He works with the grain, following the natural lines of the wood. He employs power tools in the preliminary stages of carving to cut away the bulk of the block of wood: "When I first started carving I used Tlingit or Southeastern carving tools—crooked knives. When I got to doing larger things I started using gouges of all different sizes, pounding them with mallets." Hoover relied on an adze when he first started carving, but later turned to electric saws to cut away large portions of the wood and using crooked knives for more detailed work.

Hoover has a deep respect for his material and loves every part of working with wood.

> As a child I helped my widowed mother cut wood for our stove. We cut wood in the winter so we could more easily move it to our house on sleds. I whittled firestarters every night out of the driest pieces. These were the substitute for paper to start the fires, as there was very little paper to burn. Wood has always been important to me. The agelessness and beauty of wood, the many different varieties, smells and, of course, the varied densities which make each wood a different challenge to carve and sculpt.[15]

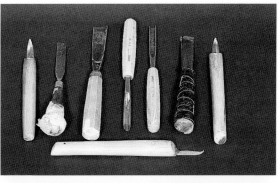

Fig. 29. *Handmade carving tool used by John Hoover.*

Fig. 30. *John Hoover's carving tools (ancient).*

Fig. 31. *John Hoover's carving tools (modern).*

BREAK FROM TRADITION

After working with traditional Northwest images for many of his first works in wood, Hoover began to resist the formal restrictions he thought came hand-in-hand with the style. He began to perceive these conventions as rigid and wanted more spontaneity. So he set out to create something new, founded in tradition, but inspired by his own imagination. "I guess the change was simply artist's prerogative," Hoover said. "I was tired of all the rules in traditional carving. Everything had to be the same. So I broke off to find my own style, like the Cubists or the Impressionists before them."[16]

The Northwest Coast art tradition is identified by continuous, broad formlines that define and outline areas within a design, or sometimes the entire design, forming a grid over the entire decorated area.[17] Formline elements become patterns, or templates, for the creation of art. Representational forms such as eyes, stylized faces, beaks, claws, and tails are incorporated in designs as symbolic and immediately recognizable elements. Ancient Alaskan and Northwest carvers of bentwood boxes and utilitarian and other objects used templates like those Hoover has devised, but the traditional artists were forbidden from deviating from the templates of their particular crest or totem. "They couldn't change… an eye or a mouth or a nose," explained Hoover. While some variation is accepted today, most of traditional two-dimensional designs conform to patterns. Individual stylistic variation is found more often on such large sculptures as totem poles and houseposts. Formlines used in both painting and carving follow precise and conventionalized principles, such as split representations of animals.

Stylized images are more common in Northwest Coast art than naturalistic ones. In portraying animals, for example, designs emphasize particular parts of the body, especially the head, which is often large relative to the rest of the creature. Animals are split, sometimes at the head, sometimes at the rear, so that the creature is often shown in two profiles. Split details are not always shown in their anatomical relationship to the rest of the body; sometimes they are completely displaced. The motifs are usually symmetrical. With a simple understanding of Northwest Coast design, one can usually identify the creature being portrayed, despite its stylization.

A key aspect of composition in Northwest Coast art is the complete use of space. A creature may be arranged in the design field in a way that it is anatomically intact, but in another portrayal of the same animal it will be artistically dismembered and arranged to fill the space with little regard for anatomical linkages.[18] Creatures are often skeletonized or shown in X-ray view. Ovoid forms are sometimes used to indicate crucial joints, and the vertebral column, or spine, may be depicted as a series of connected ovoids. Ribs and other skeletal elements are also commonly portrayed.

Hoover studied these Northwest styles, but stretched to find his own imagery and iconography. He created his own patterns, based on traditional imagery, but interpreted with his own artistic vision. Hoover did keep some evidence of formline in his work in that most of his carvings include an outline that delineates the features of the animal or human figure he is representing. Most often, the outline is the raised part of the carving, creating what might be described as contour lines. The wood between the lines is carved lower and is usually a lighter shade, or another color altogether, than the lines themselves. The effect is similar to drawing, where charcoal or pencil is used to outline the outer edges of the subject and to create the lines that are imperative for understanding the subject being represented—ovals for the eyes, an outline of a nose, another oval for the mouth, two arches for the eyebrows, and so on. The rest of the drawing is shading to provide further enhancement to the shapes, to suggest depth and shadow, and to add a more artistic quality to the work. Similarly, Hoover uses color and the texture of the carving to create the artistic vision he is seeking beyond just the outline of the form. Also, like the traditional Northwest Coast styles, Hoover used stylized images rather than naturalistic ones. As his work progressed, the images would become more and more stylized and more and more recognizable as his own.

The patterns and templates created by Hoover became his storylines. He drew upon ancient Indian myths and legends for inspiration, using the stories as starting points for his carvings. The work is not meant to tell a linear tale, but rather reflects on larger themes, characters, and symbols. For Hoover, the most important thing is to create something uniquely his own:

> When I create an original, never-seen-on-earth-before piece of art, I create it out of my own conception, personal experiences, and my own self-rewarding reasons. The only rule in doing so is, when finished, it must work. It must be a true

statement of how I feel. Like a poet with words, or a dancer's choreography, the execution is the most important thing. If it works for us as artists, it works for everybody. Everybody can relate to it and recognize it as an art form.[19]

A SCULPTOR FINDS HIS FORM

In 1968 Hoover was ready for his first major sculpture show, which was held at the Collectors Gallery in Bellevue, Washington. Hoover's wife, Barbara, participated in the exhibition as well, displaying the paintings that she had created since 1963, when she had picked up John's paints and brushes while he was on a fishing trip and began her own artistic career. Her works, which combined many painting styles with Indian themes and symbols of Christianity, were included in the *50th Annual Exhibition of Northwest Artists* at the Seattle Art Museum in 1964 and won third prize in Seattle University's *5th Annual Exhibition of Religious Painting and Sculpture* the same year. The Hoovers exhibited together in several two-person shows until the couple separated in 1977.

Most of Hoover's thirty-one pieces in the Collectors Gallery exhibition were iconographic—spirit boards as well as totemic designs on false houseposts. Some carved masks were included as well. The carvings were smaller than Hoover's later work—only two or three feet in height. Hoover's houseposts were inspired by the Salish houseposts he had seen on trips to the nearby Tulalip reservation. "They were altogether different from other Northwest houseposts," recalled Hoover. "They were simple and mysterious." Hoover was experimenting with interpreting myths in this exhibition—particularly myths that he hadn't seen visually interpreted before. The work represented Hoover's early dependence on traditional forms, although he was inventing his own versions of these forms. Later, references to such traditional objects as houseposts and totems would become more obscure.

The Collectors Gallery exhibition was the validation Hoover needed for the artistic path he had chosen. The Bureau of Indian Affairs purchased all but three pieces from the exhibition for its permanent collection. The remaining three sculptures were given as gifts to visiting dignitaries by President Lyndon B. Johnson. The same works purchased by the Bureau became part of a traveling exhibition that was featured at the Edinburgh Arts Festival later the same year. The exhibition was created around the concept of the continuity of Native American art forms—showing older, traditional pieces alongside contemporary works. This was the first time such work was shown outside the Unites States and the exhibition traveled to Berlin, Santiago, Buenos Aires, and Mexico City as well as being featured in Anchorage. Curator James McGrath of the School of the Institute of American Indian Arts in Santa Fe identified Hoover as a forerunner of contemporary American Indian arts, along with other contemporary artists: Kevin Red Star, a member of the first class of the Institute of American Indian Arts during the early 1960s, who is known for his imaginative portraits of Crow Indians of the 1890s, and Nathan Jackson, a master carver of totems from Southeast Alaska.

With the money Hoover received from the Bureau's purchase, he bought a collection of Northwest Coast art that included approximately four hundred baskets and ivory carvings and several large totem poles. The collection had been owned since 1932 by Mrs. Jack Vincent, who had bought the contents of an old trading post in Edmonds. "She was a widowed lady who had this stuff down in a basement," Hoover remembered. He discovered the collection when he responded to an inquiry from Mrs. Vincent about repairing one of her totem poles. "I went down there and it [the totem pole] was lying in the alleyway, all wet. I said, 'Well, I could probably fix it, but we've got to get it some place where it will dry out. I can't glue it together like this." Vincent took Hoover to her basement where he saw an endless array of Native-crafted pieces. The collection included many utilitarian objects—knife handles, halibut hooks, sinkers and floats, hide scrapers, and such esoteric objects as seal wound plugs—carved out of stone, bone, horn, wood, and walrus ivory. There were five totem poles (artists unknown), measuring from five feet to twenty feet tall. The collection also included almost three hundred baskets from all over the United States and Alaska, two hundred ivory carvings, a bead collection, beaded bags, clothing, Eskimo bows and arrows, and some curios.

"The big doors [to the basement] opened up and it was dark down there and all I could see—it was like a dream or something. Stuff was everywhere and I said, 'My God, what is this?'" Hoover remembers. Vincent had slowly been selling the old trading post stock to collectors since 1932, when she had acquired the collection. The next day, Hoover took his five-thousand-dollar commission from his exhibition and another three thousand dollars from his fishing income and bought the entire collection, which contained artwork from many pioneer collections, primarily gathered around the turn of the century. He soon sold two of the larger totems, both ten feet tall, for four thousand dollars each, recouping his investment. Hoover still owns works from the collection, including some very rare Aleut baskets and an Eskimo ivory collection. He sees them as inspiration—a demonstration of the enduring qualities of art objects and artifacts as keepers of a culture. In acquiring the collection he hoped to preserve the objects and to allow them to be seen by others. Like his artwork, it was an effort to tell the story of ancient peoples.

Later in 1968, a choice selection of small Eskimo pieces in ivory and stone from Hoover's acquisition was exhibited at the Center for the Arts of Indian Americans in Washington, D.C., and at the Institute of American Indian Arts in Santa Fe, New Mexico. The exhibit, organized by Hoover's friend James McGrath from the Institute of American Indian Arts, was called *Quilaut*, an Eskimo word meaning "the

Fig. 32. *Walrus ivory pieces from John Hoover's collection of Northwest Coast art.*

art of getting in touch with the spirits." It was another milestone in an important professional relationship between Hoover and McGrath and the beginning of a life-long friendship.

In the late 1960s Hoover began adding panels to his spirit boards, hinging three rectangular panels together to create one unified work. The center panel was the largest, with two side panels half as wide that, when closed, would meet in the middle and cover the center panel entirely. The image shown when the panels were closed was different from the image revealed when the panels were open. Hinges allowed the sculptures to fold back in on themselves, creating alternative images and structures. *Polar Bear Spirit*, 1971 (plate 17), is one of Hoover's first triptychs in this style. On the larger center panel is the head of the polar bear, carved and painted. Rising from the base of the bear's nose, centered in the bear's forehead, is a human figure, representing the bear's spirit helper. The narrower side panels feature female figures, two stacked figures on each panel, with faces, again representing spirit helpers, carved between their legs. When closed, a sim-plified line drawing—painted, not carved—is visible, uniting the bear and the human figure as one. The melding of one creature into another reflects Hoover's interest in the ability of animal and human spirits to move between worlds through transformation.

This tripartite form became one of Hoover's signatures, although he also added the diptych form with mirrored images to his range. Eventually, almost all of his carvings were more complex than a single piece. Hoover got the idea for creating diptychs and triptychs from Russian Orthodox icons, which were known as "travel-ing" icons, because the exterior pieces folded up to protect the image inside. Hoover saw this type of Russian sculpture in his youth in Cordova, where his family occa-sionally attended a Russian Orthodox church.

In addition to making diptychs and triptychs in the late 1960s, Hoover was also creating masks and feast dishes. Based on the traditional utilitarian wooden feast dishes used by the Salish, Hoover's dishes were large and made to hang on the wall. Most were animal forms, with areas between the raised contours more deeply carved than Hoover's other works; in traditional times these divided areas would have been used for different types of food. The feast dishes are some of Hoover's simplest forms, including in their use of color. Most of the feast dishes featured the natural tones of the wood or a basic color wash.

Hoover did explore the used of color in his masks and in his diptychs and triptychs, however. When he began to work outside the classical Northwest Coast traditions, he kept the Northwest Coast colors in his work, including red, white, black, blue, and green:

> I try to use the colors that the Indians had years ago. They had ochre from a form of clay; they had white from ashes, blue from copper ore...and charcoal for black. But I didn't mix it like they did. They had a stick to poke up their nose to make it bleed and that's what they'd mix their colors with because they were real sticky and permanent. I didn't go that far.

The colors in early Northwest Coast painting were limited to a few natural pigments before the opening of trade with Europeans. Even the introduction of trade pigments did not affect the selection and use of color dramatically. The principal colors were black, red, green, blue, or blue-green. Black was derived from lignite, although at times graphite and charcoal were also used. Before the trade period, red was derived from ochers and hematite; later the Hudson's Bay Company introduced Chinese vermilion.[20] The greens and blue-greens were probably derived from copper or iron minerals. White was occasionally used in Northwest Coast art, derived from burned and pulverized clam shells.

Black was the color used most frequently, primarily for the main formlines of the design. Red was usually the secondary color, used in formlines for details, accents, and enclosures within primary designs. Blue, green, or blue-green were not always used in a design, but rather the elements that might be painted with these colors are sometimes left unpainted, producing the effect of ground or negative space. These areas are considered the third or tertiary tier of the design structure.

CREATURES AND CUTOUTS

In March 1971, John and Barbara Hoover's work was presented in a joint exhibition at the Whatcom Museum of History and Industry in Bellingham, Washington (fig. 21). The exhibition was treated as a retrospective, even though it was the first time they were introduced to the art world in a major museum exhibition. In December 1971, Barbara Hoover sold fifteen of her husband's carvings at the Old Theater Gallery in Aberdeen, Washington, while he was in Alaska fishing. The works had been created by Hoover in preparation for a solo exhibition at the Heard Museum of Anthropology and Primitive Art, scheduled for January 1972. He had to reschedule the exhibition for 1973 to allow him more time to create new work.

At this time Hoover was exploring more than his rectangular icons and feast dishes. He cut his forms out with a band saw into identifiable outlines of real and mythical creatures. Instead of rectangles, his sculptures had three-dimensional shapes: the beak of a bird, the body of a woman, or the tusks of a walrus. Throughout the remainder of his career, Hoover would only rarely return to the rectangular form after developing his cutout method.

Hoover was particularly interested in exploring mask forms. Breaking out of the traditional mask forms of a rounded face in a circular shape—as illustrated in *Salmon Woman,* 1972 (plate 21), an unpainted mask, and *Frog Spirit Mask,* 1972 (plate 23), which has a simplified facial form surrounded by radiating feathers—Hoover began to make his masks in more complex shapes, with faces transforming into animals. *Grebe Mask,* 1972 (plate 18), has a human face with two grebes rising from the temples. In *Eagle Spirit Mask,* 1972 (plate 19), an eagle begins to form from the neck of a man. Both the grebe and the eagle masks incorporate various inlays, something else Hoover was interested in at the time. *Grebe Mask* has inlaid beads for eyes, while *Eagle Spirit Mask* has ivory inlays creating the teeth and the pupils of the man. *Puffin Spirit Mask* (plate 20) incorporates a much more abstract human face, with one eye and an meandering line forming the nose and the outline of the face. From the forehead rises a puffin with a small ivory inlay human face, or spirit helper.

The grebes, eagles, and puffins featured in Hoover's masks from 1972 are common images found throughout his entire body of work. The grebe, a diving sea bird closely related to the loon, is a rare creature in other Northwest Coast or Alaskan art. Five species of grebes inhabit the Northwest Coast and Alaska, most of them migrating there in the winter. The grebe was also called upon by shaman.[21]

The eagle, on the other hand, is one of the most important beings in the art and mythology of the Northwest Coast and Alaska. It is respected for its intelligence and its power, as well as its extraordinary vision (both literally and figuratively). Eagles in myth are usually noble characters and are associated with lofty ideals and the pursuit of freedom. The bald eagle is common all along the Northwest Coast, while the golden eagle is known in the interior and in the river valleys that cut through coastal mountain ranges. Eagles are large birds of prey with exquisite hunting and fishing skills. In Northwest Coast art, a powerful beak, curving in a downward arc, identifies the eagle. Eagle is revered as a powerful hunter, but some Northwest Coast tribes occasionally hunted and ate eagles. Shamans believed in the healing powers of eagle feathers and down and used them in a variety of ceremonies and rituals.[22]

Puffins are a favorite of contemporary people of the Northwest Coast and Alaska.

The tufted puffin is the species that breeds throughout the Northwest Coast, while the horned puffin is found mostly in Alaska. Puffins are diving sea birds, and images of puffins are sometimes found on shamanic art objects symbolizing great journeys through watery realms. Puffin beaks were often used to adorn ceremonial clothing, and regalia objects such as noisemakers were attached to bentwood hoops to create ceremonial rattles.[23] Hoover often depicts puffins in his artwork, usually incorporating a side view of the animal that accentuates its colorful beak and striking appearance.

ON THE MOVE

In 1972, a busy year, Hoover moved from Edmonds to Matlock, Washington. While he had spent the summer fishing, Barbara had moved in with her mother to help her deal with the loss of her husband and subsequent battle with cancer, a battle she lost that summer. When Hoover returned from fishing, Barbara, upset from the loss of her mother, requested that the couple leave Edmonds and start over in another house and another place. She chose Matlock. Hoover described the years in Matlock as "cold, rainy and leaky," but said they enjoyed the land around their house and the horses they kept there.

Hoover received his first major award in 1972, a first place in sculpture at the *Annual Contemporary Indian Art Exhibit* at Central Washington State College. He also received a grant from the National Endowment for the Arts, which he spent teaching carving and sculpture at the Institute of American Indian Arts in Santa Fe at the invitation of James McGrath. His work was also included in a permanent exhibition at the Institute that identified six innovators, defined as Native artists who drew upon their cultural heritage while using new materials, techniques, and designs. Hoover defines an innovator as one who introduces novelty, or makes changes by introducing something new, and credits the Institute with being the first cultural organization to consider contemporary Native art an authentic art form.

During this stay at the Institute of American Indian Arts, Hoover worked with Allan Houser (1914–1994). Houser's parents, Sam and Blossom Haozous, were Warm Springs Chiricahua Apaches held as prisoners of war at Fort Sill in Oklahoma. They instilled a strong sense of history and cultural heritage in their son, who was born in Apache, Oklahoma. Houser moved to New Mexico in 1934 to study painting at the Santa Fe Indian School and became the school's most famous graduate. By 1939 he had exhibited his work in San Francisco, Washington, D.C., and Chicago. He was selected for two major mural commissions, in 1939 and 1940, for the Department of the Interior building in Washington, D.C. In 1962 Houser was asked to join the faculty of the newly created Institute of American Indian Arts. There he created the sculpture department and began focusing his own artwork on three-dimensional forms. Houser evolved a unique style of sculpture in which he assimilated experiences from his life with modern sculptural aesthetics. His influence became apparent on hundreds of students and other artists. In 1975 Houser retired from teaching to devote himself full-time to his work. In the following two decades he produced close to one thousand sculptures in stone, wood, and bronze and participated in more than fifty solo exhibitions in museums and galleries in the United States, Europe, and Asia. He worked full-time as an artist until his death in 1994.

Hoover refers to Houser as a "magician" and recalled carving with him and watching him create sculptures, as the two men stood seemingly idle, talking. Houser and Hoover had some similarities in their work: both men were interested in retaining a narrative element in their work, but while Hoover told ancient stories of Alaska and Northwest cultures, Houser focused more on the physical activities of the Apaches, rather than the mythology, depicting such activities as dancing, buffalo hunting, and praying. In the 1970s both artists were working on developing an abstracted, stylized approach to depicting human and animal figures.

Houser taught an anatomy course at the Institute using various birds and other animals as models and sketched along with the students on large pieces of newsprint. "He'd sketch this beautiful stuff in charcoal and then he'd tear it off and throw it in the garbage can," said Hoover.

> I asked him one day, "Allan, how about selling some of those sketches?" He said, "Aw, those are no good." But they were beautiful… We were about the same age, and he had been assimilated and led a life much like mine. We were good friends. I saw him the day before he died. He was still happy.

Hoover had carved some small sculptures in soapstone prior to visiting the Institute, but he attempted his first large pieces in stone while working there with Houser. Hoover created a stylized bird, similar to the birds found in his cedar carvings, and a large figurative work in serpentine stone called *Reindeer Mother*, which is displayed in his home today. "Though I will probably stay with wood, the experience of working with Allan Houser and his students was so stimulating that I continued to work in stone all winter and will do an occasional piece," he said, at the time.[24] He did not create any more works in stone, however, and looking back now, Hoover simply states, "I didn't like it. It was not my medium." In 1988 and 1990 Hoover exhibited his sculptures with his friend and mentor Houser in San Francisco and Santa Fe. In these exhibitions Hoover exhibited large bronzes, wind chimes, and mobiles, forms that eventually developed from his wood carvings.

Hoover says his experience at the Institute of the American Indian Arts helped him to branch out artistically. His work became more stylized and abstracted. He enjoyed the camaraderie he developed with the other artists who were there at the same time, including Allan Houser, Charles Loloma, and Fritz Scholder. "I think we influenced each other a lot," said Hoover. "Not so much in obvious ways when you look at our art, but more because we encouraged each other to grow and because we all accepted one another's art. We agreed about what art was."

RECOGNITION AND SUCCESS

Hoover's 1973 exhibition at the Heard Museum, as rescheduled, was shared with painter Franklin Fireshaker, a Ponca painter from Ojai, California. The exhibition was a critical point for Hoover. It was a large exhibition, including more than thirty works. Hoover was working larger than he had previously, creating six- to eight-foot carvings of spirit birds, which he called "souls in flight" and which represented the flight of a shaman while in a trance. He created most of the work for the exhibition after his experience teaching and working at the Institute of the American Indian in Santa Fe. "My work was changing then," said Hoover. "I was all hyped up with new ideas."

While Hoover was still creating spirit boards similar to those he made before Santa Fe, the designs had grown more ambitious. *Spirit Board*, 1973 (plate 24), is a sixty-inch cedar plank on which Hoover carved and painted a visual timeline showing the progression of a boy's life from birth to death. At the bottom of the piece a child is born. As the boy grows old, a man with a red cane comes to claim him and takes him across the river into spirit world. This is some of Hoover's most complicated imagery and one of the only linear storylines he has attempted to portray. *Raven People*, 1972 (plate 22), is less complicated, but still more ornate than his early work. Two figures are stacked on the six-foot cedar plank. The figure at the top is foreboding, with a dark face, circled eyes, and bared teeth. The lower figure is more innocent and less threatening. Hoover was still using some inlay at this time, embedding small pieces of ivory for the figures' eyes.

The Heard Museum bought six works from Hoover's 1973 exhibition for their permanent collection. Hoover recalls that one critic wrote that the work in the exhibition was "too esoteric for most people." Sandra Day O'Connor, a Supreme Court justice and once a congresswoman from Arizona, bought two of Hoover's triptychs from the exhibition (the Heard Museum later named a wing of the museum after her). "We corresponded a couple of times; got some neat letters from her," said Hoover.

Also in 1973, one of Hoover's woodcarvings, entitled *Salmon Woman*, won the second-place award at the Heard Museum's *Sculpture I* American Indian competition. *Salmon Woman*, 1972 (fig. 33), a figure Hoover had begun while teaching at the Institute of American Indian Arts, was created from a slab of red cedar after Hoover's friend, Nick Spanovick, related to Hoover the story of Salmon Woman he had heard. Spanovick was a machinest working in a cannery in Ketchikan who also sharpened tools for Alaskan totem pole carver Jones "Skultas" Yeltatsie. Yeltatsie took Spanovick down to a river in Ketchikan to show him some ancient petroglyphs

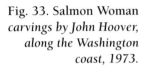

Fig. 33. *Salmon Woman carvings by John Hoover, along the Washington coast, 1973.*

representing Salmon Woman. Spanovick made rubbings from the petroglyphs, which he later showed to Hoover as he retold the legend he'd heard from Yeltatsie.

Salmon Woman is one of the more significant supernatural figures identified with the arctic and the lower regions of the Northwest Coast, including Washington, Oregon, and northern California. Salmon Woman was considered to be a guardian spirit to both shamans and the community. All along the coast, people's stories tell of Salmon Woman's gift of food for the people. Sacred narratives tell of the Salmon People who lived at the bottom of the sea in longhouses like those of people in the villages. The Salmon People only put on their salmon robes when it was time for them to make the annual salmon run. When the salmon swam from the sea toward the rivers, the people along the rivers would sing songs and thank the salmon for sacrificing themselves as food for the people. Salmon bones were offered by people facing downriver so that the salmon spirits could return to the sea and become fish once again. The salmon were a link between two worlds.

Natives of the Northwest Coast have depended upon salmon runs as a food source for centuries. The fish serves as a powerful symbol of regeneration, self-sacrifice, and perseverance. Shortages of salmon are traditionally attributed to human disrespect and refusal to live by the wisdom of the elders. Salmon are honored and celebrated by all coastal peoples, often in the form of Salmon Woman:

> Salmon Woman, which I do a lot of, that's a myth. They [Alaska Natives] used to put salmon women at the head of every fish stream in the village so that the fish would always return. They were a form of petroglyphs, but they had been represented as salmon women who had big breasts and were very beautiful, so the salmon could not resist her—they had to come back every year to spawn there.

In 1974 Hoover and his wife moved to Grapeview, Washington, overlooking Pickering Passage and Hartstene Island on the southern extremes of Puget Sound, where Hovoer has now lived for the last twenty-five years in a home he calls "the place that looks down on birds." Hoover developed this property into an ideal setting for life and art, building a studio just steps from the house and then adding a deck and bathhouse overlooking the water.

Hoover traveled abroad in 1974, visiting Japan, Taiwan, and the Philippines, hired as part of an artist-in-residence program with the school system that educated the children of U.S. Armed Services men and women. Hoover spent two weeks in each country, living in the Air Force officers' barracks while in each location. Time in between the residencies was spent traveling around the countries and visiting small villages. The experience reinforced his desire to celebrate his culture through his art:

> I spent some time as a visiting artist in the Orient. I marveled at the Japanese temples—beautiful, elaborate structures made by priests. I found Filipino and Taiwanese woodworkers to be master craftsmen, capable of reproducing an image exactly as they saw it with great precision, and I learned their carving techniques just by watching. I found only one man making ancestor figures, much like those of the ancient Eskimos, and resembling those I was then carving. I felt that I was helping to revive an almost lost art.[25]

Most of the villages Hoover visited in Taiwan had ancestor figures at their entrances. These were ancient carvings that had survived for generations. They represented fertility and were in place to bring good luck to the village. Contemporary carvers were not permitted to carve replicas of the figures; they were sacred. Hoover, however, carved his own ancestor figure when he returned home to his Washington studio and it was a theme he would repeat later.

In 1974 Hoover's cedar triptych *Otter Daughter* took the first award in sculpture at the Philbrook Museum of Art's Annual American Indian Artists Exhibition in Tulsa, Oklahoma. The sea otter had become a favorite image of Hoover and many other artists in the Northwest. Sea otters are believed to be important arbiters of morality and human behavior, withdrawing their support from hunters who do not honor their sacrifice to die at the hunter's hand in order to feed his village. Sea otters are challenging prey and hunting them was a prestigious activity. Otters are known to be highly intelligent, resourceful, and agile, able to use their forepaws like hands. Otters are also very playful, a characteristic that has identified otter images as symbols of laughter and lightheartedness.[26] The sea otter was often depicted floating on its back, grasping a shell or a sea urchin. *Whale and Otter Sprit,* 1975 (plate 28), is a triptych mask form in which a human face incorporates the shape of a whale; two otters form the hinged panels on each side.

The Aleuts had at least eleven legends about the origin of the sea otter and many tales about hunting them. Otter figurines made in the Aleutians were sometimes used as adornments on Aleut kayaks, hunting hats, floats, and throwing boards. Such fine and intricate objects made by man were thought to attract sea mammals, especially otters, who were believed to be transformed humans.[27]

The sea otter also has a negative association related to the forced conscription of the Aleuts by the Russians, but this history also adds to the spiritual power of the animal. Hoover told the following history:

> The Aleuts were masters at hunting sea mammals, and the Russians were aware of their prowess…The Russians would transfer the Aleut hunters with their kayaks aboard ship from their villages out to the open seas where otters were found. The Russians never admitted that the Aleuts were deprived of their human rights when forced to hunt. The traders left the Aleuts to survive as best they could in skin boats. The result is that hunters would often be too long at sea, and the kayaks would collapse around them, and they would drown. Sometimes they were left so long at the hunting grounds, immobilized in their kayaks, that their legs would develop gangrene and would later have to be amputated. On other occasions, if the hunters refused to leave their villages to hunt the otters, the Russians would line up the males and see how many they could shoot with a single bullet. The greed of the Russian fur traders for otter pelts put the animal on the brink of extinction. It also brought on the near demise of the Aleut hunters and their families and villages. The Aleuts were conscripted from every island and village the Russians could locate.[28]

Despite this sad history, Hoover reveres the otter for the important place it held in Aleut society before its role was tainted by the Russians.

In 1975 Hoover received first and second awards at the Heard Museum Guild's Annual Indian Arts and Crafts Exhibition. At this time, he was again exploring the mask form but now, instead of showing humans transforming into animals with one-piece cutouts, he was adding appendages to elaborated mask forms. *Salmon Man*, 1974 (plate 25), features a human face in the center of the large shape of an animal. Attached to the sides are two salmon: the one on the left facing upstream, the one on the right facing downstream. The salmon are attached to the central mask figure by two small sticks, expanding the mask form into more complicated sculpture.

In 1977 Hoover received a first award in wood sculpture, again at the Heard Museum Guild's *Annual Indian Arts and Crafts Exhibition*. In February 1978 Hoover and his son Tony, then twenty-nine-years old and a painter, presented a father-and-son exhibition at the Haines Gallery in Seattle. Tony, who now lives in Ballard, Washington, is a watercolor painter, creating landscapes and wildlife paintings along with works inspired by science fiction.

Hoover was still continuing to fish in Alaska each summer at this time, although he no longer was financially dependent upon it. Instead, he felt it was meaningful and good for his soul, describing fishing as the thing he knew best.

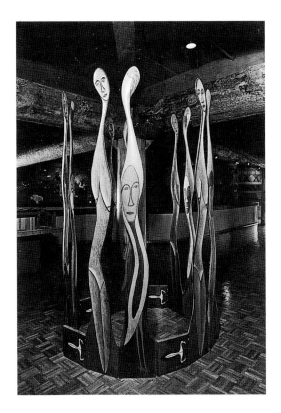

Fig. 34. Winter Loon Dance, *1981. Installation at the Daybreak Star Center, Seattle, Washington.*

GOING PUBLIC

In 1977 Hoover received his first and second public art commissions, the beginning of what became an important outlet for his creativity and a source of financial support. The first commission was one of Hoover's most noted public art installations: *Ancestor Figures* (fig. 25), an indoor sculpture created for the Daybreak Star Center in Seattle. Eight feet tall by twelve feet wide, it depicts Salmon, Killer Whale, Wolf, Eagle, and Raven—representing crests found in Southeast Alaskan Indian cultures. Another Hoover sculpture is permanently installed at the Daybreak Star Center as well, although it was not intended as a piece of public art. In a 1981 group exhibition at the Daybreak Star Center, comedian Richard Pryor saw Hoover's work while he was taking a lunch break from shooting a film nearby. The piece Pryor saw at the exhibition was *Winter Loon Dance* (fig. 34), which depicted eight dancing loons through combinations of bird and human elements.

> Pryor came in during the lunch hour and saw that piece, *Winter Loon Dance*. It's about nine feet high and about ten feet in diameter and is probably made up of a dozen pieces . He said, "I want that, how much is that?" "Four thousand dollars." He said, "Okay, I'll take it and I want to take it with me when I leave tonight." They couldn't do that. They couldn't pack it up that quickly. So he said, "Okay, you [Daybreak Star Center] keep it." And it's still there.

In 1978 Hoover created a large mobile (measuring nine feet tall by nine feet wide) for the King County Alcoholic Center in Seattle based on the supernatural being Sedna, the Great Goddess of the Alaska Inuit, or Inupiat (fig. 35). This was Hoover's first exploration of the mobile, a form whose potential for animating a large public space allowed him to move beyond two-dimensional wall hangings. He also chose the mobile form because it lent itself well to the theme he had chosen: Sedna,

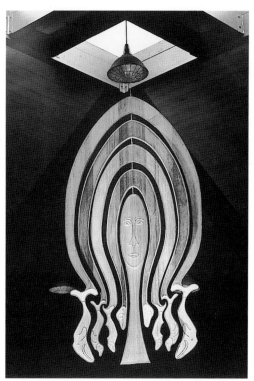

Fig. 35. Sedna *(mobile)*, 1978. Installation at the King County Alcoholic Treatment Center.

a water-spirit and the archetypal figure of Inuit mythology, and some of the creatures that make up Sedna's undersea world.

Many Native peoples honor an earth goddess, but the Inuit, whose survival depends on the sea, have elevated Sedna. She shares aspects of a great goddess as conceived by other groups and has an ambivalent nature, being simultaneously the source of all life and ruler of the dead.

Sedna was born to two giants and immediately proved to have an insatiable appetite that grew so large that one night she started to devour her sleeping parents. The terrified parents snatched up the infant and carried her to their umiak (a large hunting boat) and paddled far out to the sea, where they threw her overboard. Sedna clung to the sides of the canoe until her parents cut off her fingers, and she sank beneath the waves. There she became the ruler of the ocean, governing both the sea and all its creatures, who were born from her severed fingers.

When Inuit hunters were unable to find any prey, their shaman sent his spirit down to plead with Sedna. To reach her home, the shaman's spirit had to first pass through the land of the dead and a treacherous, icy whirlpool. Next, the spirit had to pass an enormous cauldron full of boiling seals, evade the fierce guard-dog of Sedna, and then cross an abyss on a knife-thin edge, before arriving at Sedna's palace. There, the spirit danced for Sedna, hoping to induce her into helping his people. Sedna might instruct the shaman's spirit to build a new settlement, or she would agree to send them seals and other prey. Some arctic people, including the Bering Sea Inupiat, performed a ritual ceremony called the Bladder Festival to placate Sedna so that she would release the marine mammals she held captive. They would inflate bladders of the animals they hunted and float them out to sea.

The Inuit had no visual representation of Sedna. They believed that to create her image was sacrilegious and would offend Sedna for she might believe the people were trying to steal her soul. In modern days, Sedna has been popularly portrayed by Inuit artists and others as a half-human, half-sea creature, with the sea creature usually taking the form of a whale, seal, walrus, or fish, probably because legend says that Sedna was once a human who then became a sea dweller.

The King County project was not Hoover's first—or last—depiction of Sedna. Most of his depictions show a human form in the process of transforming into a sea mammal, such as a walrus or an otter. The human face of Sedna can be found within the body of the animal, such as between the tusks of the walrus, or the animal can be found within the human form of Sedna, such as between her legs. In his King County mobile, Hoover features Sedna along with all of her sea creatures, including whales, seals, and fish. He said he did not depict a specific story about Sedna, but was simply trying to portray her as a powerful goddess. A year after the mobile was installed, a group of the center's residents threw cups at the sculpture during their lunch hour. The effort knocked the sculpture down from the ceiling, breaking it irreparably. The sculpture was never replaced.

Hoover's personal life underwent some changes during this time. He separated from his wife Barbara in 1977 and soon met Mary Rockness in Cordova. Like Hoover, Mary had been involved in the Alaskan salmon fisheries for more than twenty years. They married in 1978 and decided to make Grapeview their permanent home.

A NEW DECADE

In 1979 Hoover returned to Alaska for a solo exhibition at the Anchorage Museum of History and Art. Hoover identifies this exhibition as one of his career highlights and still feels grateful to the Anchorage Museum for the support the institution has given him over the years. "I could kiss their feet," said Hoover. "At my solo exhibition everyone was very supportive and very sincere. It's very rewarding for an artist to have people who show an interest in and a respect for their work."

The artwork presented in this exhibition—and later, in 1982, in Night of the First Americans, a one-night exhibition of the work of four hundred Native artists and reception hosted by the Kennedy Center in Washington, D.C.—was very symmetrical and stylized. Hoover's diptych and triptych forms were cutouts and relied on repetitive shapes and images. The cutouts were also growing increasingly more complex, along with the ability of the sculptures to transform when the hinged panels were opened and closed. For example, an elegant loon on the exterior of a closed sculpture transforms into two loon spirit helpers and two men when the piece is unfolded, as illustrated here in *Blind Man and the Loon,* 1980 (plate 31).

The figures that were featured on the center panels of the triptychs were now most often women, made obvious with breasts that created an irregular shape for the outline of the sculptures. *Puffin Spirit,* 1980 (plate 30), is one example of the central female figure. Two puffins frame her, with their chests conforming to the shape of her neck, shoulders, and head. The puffins' beaks rise above her head, pointing upward. Two other puffins, one on each side, complete the triptych form, meeting the other puffins back to back.

For Hoover, the feminine form is used to represent elemental sources of life. Hoover's literature on shamans revealed the awe accorded to women for their ability to give birth. The shamans believed this ability gave women one of nature's secrets that they themselves could never possess. Ancient shamans also believed that the act of creation was a feminine act and thus tried to carry out their own activities in an androgynous manner to successfully make the journey into the supernatural world.

Hoover finds that women are not just represented in his work, they are particularly drawn to it:

> A lot of women buy my work. I don't know what it is. Maybe because I use the female form, or...the reason I use that is because in Siberia some shamans were women, and the women were the most important shamans, the most powerful.

They had an easier...access to the spirit world and created work that was more important. Even the men dressed as women to try to get that power. I use the woman form a lot.

By the early 1980s Hoover was again playing with variations on his sculptural forms. His mask shapes with appendages had become more fluid, as illustrated in *Loon Man Soul Catcher,* 1980 (plate 33). Now the central mask figure was almost unrecognizable as a mask, although the human face in the center is still present. The face is framed by another circle that is surrounded again by a two-headed loon form. Human figures are the appendages, curving along the sides of the sculpture, molded to imitate the circular shapes.

A soul catcher, in most Northwest Coast cultures, was a tubular implement used by a shaman to capture the soul of a sick person when it left the body at dusk. The soul catcher would cleanse the captured soul and return it in a healthy state to the patient. Although Hoover uses the term *soul catcher* in many titles for his art-work, as in *Loon Man Soul Catcher*, the form he sculpts is not consistent with the idea of the soul catcher as an implement or tool. Hoover is more interested in depicting soul catchers as animals, or the spirits of animals, who assist the shaman in retriev-ing souls. Loons are the animals Hoover most often chooses for the task, as they served as guardian spirits to the Aleut shamans.

An Aleut story tells of a man receiving restorative powers from a loon by riding on its back as it swims beneath the sea. As a marine bird, the loon unites the worlds of sky and water; this ability to bridge two worlds makes it an ideal subject for transformation. The loon was believed to be able to penetrate deep into the under-sea world by diving to significant depths while hunting for fish. The loon also was an important bird because it warned people of coming storms.[29]

When Hoover was growing up in Cordova, loons would fly out in the morning from Eyak Lake across to the saltwater bay on the other side of the town. In the evening they would return to the lake. The Eyaks, the tribe that lived for two thou-sand years on the lake, believed that the loon was part human because it had what the Eyaks called "round rumps" with no tail feathers, so the loons were not hunted or eaten by the Eyaks. Hoover recalls fishing one day in the Copper River flats, drifting along, when he heard a noise. It was a loon flying around the boat, squawk-ing. When Hoover pulled up his net, there were two loons in it that had drowned, a male and a female. One had been the first to die; the other, unable to save its mate, had joined it in death. Hoover believes the loon was calling to him for help. Hoover felt remorse for the lost birds and has since identified loons as his spirit helpers. In the 1980s loons were a dominant subject matter for Hoover, including *Loon Woman,* 1980 (plate 34), a panel carving depicting a woman with a loon rising from each side of her body (the loons themselves also have feminine bodies); *Red-Throated*

Fig. 36. *John Hoover on Rialto Beach, Washington, 1976, with* Seaweed People *carvings.*

Loon Spirit Mask, 1984 (plate 40), a triptych with a simple face surrounded by two pairs of symmetrical loons; and *Underwater Loon Woman*, 1985 (plate 46), a face with a loon rising high from each side of the temples, becoming asymmetrical at the top of the carving, one with its beak open, the other with its beak closed.

NEW MATERIALS

By the 1980s Hoover was using artist oil colors and mixing them with turpentine and linseed oil to add color to his artwork. The additives thin the paint out to a stainlike substance that Hoover then applies with a brush, later rubbing it in with a cloth until the grain shows through. Hoover feels it gives the work an old, patinaed look. Hoover's signature colors—washes of orange, rust, wood tones, the blue-greens of the sea—accent the natural tones of the red cedar.

In 1981 Hoover created a hanging sculpture—his first mobile form since *Sedna* for the King County public commission—called *Octopus Chimes* (plate 35). This is a large work, with four layered cedar forms, shaped like horseshoes, each section smaller than the next so that they hang inside one another. These suggest eight tentacles, like those of an octopus, as the name of the piece suggests. The same sculpture was later cast in bronze.

Hoover was intrigued with the visual effect of casting his carved works in metal. He enjoyed seeing his sculptures recast into a new material, at first mostly casting pre-existing works. He appreciated the durability of the metal and was interested in the subtle changes bronze brought to forms he had carved in cedar. While his first works in bronze were cast from his cedar carvings, he now makes the molds from foam because the original cedar works rarely survived the casting process.

A sculpture called *Seaweed People* (fig. 36) was the first work to be cast. Hoover's friend and collector Dave Kalamar saw a small four-foot version of *Seaweed People* carved in cedar one day in 1982 when he was visiting Hoover's studio. Kalamar inquired whether Hoover had ever considered casting his work in bronze. When Hoover said no, Kalamar pointed at *Seaweed People* and said, "Make that twice as big and cast it in bronze and I'll buy it." Hoover carved a larger form in cedar and had the sculpture cast at the Seattle-area River Dog Foundry.

Seaweed People was quickly followed by *Blue Jay*, 1982, and then a series of rattles. Hoover's rattles are based on raven rattles, a standard accoutrement of a Northwest Coast chief that were used in ceremonies. The different sounds and rhythms produced by a pair of rattles enhanced the drama of a chief's oratory. While the basic form of a traditional rattle is that of Raven holding a small object in his beak, refering to the myth of the bird bringing sunlight to mankind, Hoover more often created rattles in the shape of puffins than in Raven's image.

Hoover also created *Hummingbird Feeder*, 1982 (plate 37), in bronze, which, like *Octopus Chimes*, was meant to be an outdoor sculpture that could interact with the wind. *Hummingbird Feeder*, *Octopus Chimes*, and *Sedna* all demonstrate Hoover's interest in making sculptures that do not rise from the ground, but rather hang from the ceiling, creating possibilities for movement.

In 1983 Hoover traveled to Lincoln, Nebraska, for an exhibition at the Sheldon Jackson Memorial Art Gallery. He installed his work himself and remembers taking down an Alexander Calder mobile in the gallery's lobby to install one of his own works (Hoover's work is back on display in the same spot today). In deinstalling the Calder mobile, Hoover became intrigued with the form and balance of Calder's work. "It was massive, beautiful, always moving," recalled Hoover. When he returned home to his own studio, Hoover experimented further with the mobile form and its potential in his work. In 1985 he constructed *Shaman's Tree of Life* (plate 36), now part of the permanent collection of the Anchorage Museum of History and Art. In this work, rather than having the mobile hang from the ceiling, Hoover created his own version of a mobile, with a free-standing base, almost like a coat rack, from which a series of five birds rotate in a totem-like structure. From each wing of each bird, small human figures dangle from twine strung with trading beads. The sculpture is meant to represent the many birds that were most important to the shaman. Different birds, as spirit helpers, had different powers. The shaman depended on all these powers to heal his or her people and to enter the spirit world.

In 1984 Hoover received a commission for what would become his favorite public art installation. *Volcano Woman* consists of thirteen figures, with the central figure of Volcano Woman surrounded by eight female figures (guardian spirits) forming an outer circle, and four cormorants making up an inner circle (fig. 37). Cormorants are diving sea birds, whose ability to both fly in the air and move

Fig. 37. Volcano Woman,
1984. Installation at the
William A. Egan
Convention Center.

underwater accounts for their appearance in shamanic contexts in Northwest and Alaskan cultures, as shamans often seek the guidance of creatures that can move from one environment to another. Hoover is pleased with the way this sculpture fills a seating area in the building and the complexity of the interaction of the forms.

Volcano Woman, in Northwest Coast culture, is the protector of the forest. People must respect Volcano Woman, as she protects all wild creatures as her children. Volcano Woman is volatile, vengeful, and violent at times. According to Lydia T. Black, a scholar of Aleut art and culture, only one Aleut story of Volcano Woman has been documented in writing, and no images of Volcano Woman exist from ancient times.[30] Rather, Volcano Woman was described through oral traditions, from generation to generation. Hoover's depiction of Volcano Woman, however, combines the Aleut text (referred to by Black) and versions of the story from oral traditions with his own imagination. The story of Volcano Woman seeks to explain how the Aleutian Islands of Alaska were populated. Hoover recounted the story in this way:

> Volcanoes were being formed in the Aleutians, and the volcanoes formed islands. A flock of cormorants went by one volcano and a beautiful woman emerged, the Volcano Woman. So they all stopped and changed into human form and mated with her and then changed back into cormorants. But they flew their babies all over the islands, and, in this way, the islands became populated.

Hoover believes that his is the first visual interpretation of the Volcano Woman story by an artist. Each of the three separate, but interrelated, circular elements is a different color, which Hoover says reflect natural earth tones: grays, greens, and reds. The simple, plain carving on the backsides of the figures is consistent with the Northwest Coast tradition, which usually left the backs of totem poles, mortuary poles, and other ceremonial sculptures unadorned.

To carve the sculpture, Hoover selected a single three-hundred-year-old cedar log and had it planed into boards of varying thicknesses, as required for each element of the composition. Saws were used to take the boards down to their rough shapes, and then they were sculpted by hand with a series of woodcarving gouges. Hoover worked for six months in his Grapeview studio carving the legend into life before it was installed at the William A. Egan Civic and Convention Center in Anchorage. Of his public commissions Hoover said with a wink, "No one has gotten mad at my public art yet. Even the naked ones like *Volcano Woman*. Maybe I'm not provocative enough."[31]

In the mid-1980s Hoover returned to some simpler sculptural forms. *Salmon Women,* 1985, is a diptych with two salmon hinged at the back and at the tail. Inside each of the salmon are two androgynous figures. The color, too, is subtle, with light shades of orange and green. *Salmon People,* 1985 (plate 38), is a similar work, with two fish, showing their sharpened teeth, enclosing the shapes of two female figures. Here the color is even more subtle, with much of the wood left natural and the rest of the work in shades of brown. *Walrus Spirit Mask,* 1985 (plate 43), shows a return to Hoover's cutout mask forms. Here, the circular face of a walrus is only disrupted by two tusk shapes that protrude from the center. *Underwater Loon Woman,* 1985 (plate 46), has a female head with two loons rising from the nape of her neck. The form is again simple, although this time Hoover has made the repeated shapes asymmetrical, with one loon shorter than the other.

NEW BEGINNINGS

By 1986 Hoover was experimenting with more complex structures for his artwork. *Kingfisher Spirit* (plate 47) features a more jagged cutout edge, inspired by the spiked head feathers of the kingfisher. Kingfishers are straight-billed, colorful, crested shorebirds with excellent fishing skills. Kingfisher is considered a useful spirit guide by the people of the Northwest Coast because it is at home in various environments and quite solitary and resourceful. Hoover's kingfisher depiction features a strong, straight beak and a short tail. In other Northwest Coast art, kingfishers are commonly depicted with a fish in its beak or talons.[32] The side panels of Hoover's triptych are identical to each other, as in most of Hoover's earlier triptychs, but this time one is flipped upside-down, a prelude to Hoover's later experiments with more asymmetrical forms.

Hoover's work from the late 1980s is marked by spirit masks with a centerpiece surrounded by multiple, repeated carvings of another form—such as human figures, salmon, or birds. The carved forms that radiate out from the central carving recall the feathers that were placed around Yup'ik style masks in ancient times. *Salmon Man,* 1987 (plate 50), is one such example, with a complicated facial image of hu-

Fig. 38. Portrait of John Hoover *by Alvin Amason, friend and fellow Aleut artist.*

man figures and salmon surrounded by eight human figures. Hoover continued to experiment with his mask forms with appendages during the late 1980s. *Aleut Hunter Spirit Mask,* 1987 (plate 52), features the face of an otter, with a spirit helper balanced atop his forehead. On each side, two Aleut hunters with bentwood hats and spears, seated in kayaks, face the otter.

Hoover was also constructing more freestanding works during this time. *Frog and Heron,* 1987 (plate 51), is a four-foot-tall carved heron standing on the flattened form of a frog, which serves as the base for the sculpture. Frogs appear only occasionally in Hoover's work. When used, they most often have a secondary role as companions to another animal he is depicting. As an amphibian that lives in two worlds, water and land, the frog is admired for its adaptability, knowledge, and the power to traverse and inhabit diverse realms, both natural and supernatural.[33] Frogs are primary spirit helpers of shamans.

Salmon Woman, 1987 (plate 53), is similar to *Frog and Heron,* although more ambitious in its form. A female figure is suspended from a base with two bear heads by two partial wolf forms. Salmon protrude from her hips and a cluster of eggs decorates her belly. Hoover incorporated all of these animals, as well as the human figure, to suggest all these creatures' dependence upon the salmon for food. The sculptures called *Loon Children,* 1989 (plate 57), and *Swan Spirit,* 1988 (plate 54), are also free-standing works from this period.

The early 1990s saw a continuation of these themes in Hoover's work. Most works from this time have a minimal use of color, with mostly natural tones, as in *Seal Child,* 1990 (plate 63), and *Loon Spirit,* 1991 (plate 66). Many of the works are large freestanding works such as *And You Thought You Were Pregnant,* 1992 (plate 69), and *That's What You Get for Horsing Around,* 1993 (plate 72). Both of these works include hinges and are made up of two pieces. The hinges are not to create a diptych, however, but to provide Hoover with a wider surface area. The hinges are not functional as hinges because the works are attached to a base and do not have the ability to fold and unfold. One of Hoover's favorite works from this time is *Aleut Storyboard: Old Man of the Sea,* 1993 (plate 68), another reference to the Aleut's dependence upon the sea otter.

By the early 1990s Hoover's life was almost entirely dedicated to art, rather

Fig. 39. Seaweed People, *installed at the White House, Washington, D.C. 1998.*

Fig. 40. *Hillary Clinton, Mary Hoover, John Hoover, and Anna Hoover inside the White House, Washington, D.C., 1997.*

than split between art and fishing. Hoover continued to fish in Alaska every summer until 1993 when he finally retired from this laborious work. The tradition does continue, however: Hoover's wife Mary and daughter Anna continue to own and operate a commercial fishing boat out of Bristol Bay.

In the mid-1990s, Hoover experimented with asymmetrical triptychs, adding another layer to the folding and unfolding of his sculptures. He also added brighter colors as well as metallic paints—particularly copper. *Loon Lady,* 1994 (plate 75), is an asymmetrical triptych. In the center is a dancing female figure. On her left side are two shorter loons painted in purple; on her right are two larger, two-toned brown loons. Each set of loons mirrors one another, but the sets are not identical, creating an asymmetrical effect. *Loon People,* 1996 (plate 82), is another asymmetrical triptych. The loon makes up the center of the sculpture, looking up at one of the two white female figures on its left. Those figures stand back-to-back, with their heads tilting away from one another. On the loon's right, two more figures stand, with both heads tilting toward the loon. One of the figures is female, while the other is a male with a bright orange torso.

Blue Jay Man, Self-Portrait, 1995 (plate 77), is one of few self-portraits Hoover created in his career. In the center is the artist wearing a leather cord strung with a human figure sculpted in ivory, similar to necklaces often worn by Hoover. When the sculpture is closed, the face of the artist is encircled by two blue jays; when open, four blue jays accompany the artist. Hoover chose the blue jay for this personal triptych because he has always identified with the bird—in part because his middle name is Jay. The local blue jay, known as the Stellar's Jay, is a chatty, active bird that is common along the Northwest Coast and is related to crows and ravens. It is also a frequent visitor to Hoover's Grapeview home. Like Raven, the blue jay is a trickster in the mythologies of Salish cultures. Hoover, who is known for his joke telling, feels an affinity to the blue jay in this way as well.

In 1995 Hoover was chosen to participate in an international traveling exhibition organized by the Heard Museum. He contributed one sculpture, a large bird form called *Shaman in the Form of an Eagle,* to the exhibition, which included works by more than two hundred artists. He and his family accompanied his work to New Zealand, where he was deeply moved by a visit to Wangahui, one of the older Maori settlements. Hoover met with Maori tribes and was honored at numerous ceremonies.

In 1997 the Heard Museum selected twelve contemporary Indian artists to show their work in the sculpture garden of the White House. By tradition, begun by Jackie Kennedy, this exhibition was sponsored by the First Lady. Hillary Clinton continued Joan Mondale's program of displaying American art in the White House. She featured art from a different area of the nation, each year replacing the sculptures in the Kennedy Garden with new work. The Heard Museum did not own an outdoor piece by Hoover, so the artist had another bronze edition of *Seaweed People,* previously cast in 1982, made specifically for the exhibition (fig. 39).

The installation of American Indian sculpture, displayed in the Jacqueline Kennedy Gardens from November 1997 through September 1998, was the first exclusively Native American selection, which Clinton noted in the brochure. "Visitors to the White House will be reminded of the irreplaceable contributions of Native Americans. I hope this celebration of our country's creative spirit will enable each of us to gain a greater appreciation of the vibrant cultural traditions we share as a nation and as a people," Clinton wrote in the exhibition catalogue.

Seaweed People is a visualization of the spirit helpers who assist the Aleut people. This image of humanistic seaweed forms comes not from ancient stories, but from Hoover's imagination. "The Seaweed People are just my idea," said Hoover. "...Natives that live on the coast, on the salt water, depended upon seaweed for years. That was their Safeway store. They gathered seaweed and made everything out of it. If you have ever seen bull kelp, swaying and dancing with the currents, you can see what it is I was trying to portray in this sculpture."

Hoover says the pinnacle of his career, thus far, was in 1998 when he created a monumental bronze sculpture of Raven, titled *Raven the Creator* (fig. 41), for the Alaska Native Heritage Center in Anchorage. Hoover chose the image of Raven for the sculpture because this animal is identified as the original Creator in much of Native American mythology, and he wanted something that could represent all the Natives of Alaska. Hoover added elements from different legends about Raven to his sculpture, especially the iconography of stealing the Box of Daylight, in which the Old Man of the Nass, in Tlingit legend, kept the celestial bodies. Stars dangle from Raven's beak, and the sun and the moon hang from each wing. The human figures

Fig. 41. Raven the Creator, *installed at the Alaska Native Heritage Center in Anchorage, 1998.*

in his claws resemble the triptych icons used by the Orthodox faithful in Aleut regions. The human face in the belly of Raven represents Mother Earth, and the face at the back of the head of Raven is symbolic of the many transformations made by Raven.

"It was rewarding to get that commission," said Hoover, "I think nine other Alaska Native artists applied for it." Hoover submitted a sketch to the public art committee, which made the selections of artwork for the brand-new cultural center in Anchorage. When the proposal was accepted, Hoover immediately went to work on one of his biggest and most challenging projects.

> We had to make the damn raven from a sketch and it was quite a challenge. We got a block of foam ten feet long, five feet wide, and two feet thick that weighed 500 pounds. We made templates from the original sketch and enlarged them and then started cutting away at the foam. It took us six weeks to get the 'plug,' as they call it. And they took the plug to the foundry and cut it all up into pieces and cast them individually and then welded them all back together. Took them four months to do it—and forty thousand bucks.

A Grapeview neighbor and friend, Jim Knull, worked with Hoover to sculpt the foam. Knull is a trained woodworker who makes sculpted furniture. The job was messy. "Any time you touched the foam, the powder, like sugar, would just fly up in the air. And we didn't wear masks or anything. It was quite 'icky,'" said Hoover. He was exceedingly pleased with the results, however. "It turned out so good, it was amazing," he mused. "And all, most Natives in Alaska can relate to it. It's a striking piece. Sometimes I can't believe we did that." The image of the thirteen-foot-high bronze sculpture was used by the Census Bureau on posters and T-shirts to encourage Alaska Natives and others in rural Alaskan areas to participate in Census 2000.

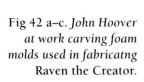

Fig 42 a–c. *John Hoover at work carving foam molds used in fabricatng* Raven the Creator.

TODAY

In the late 1990s Hoover was creating unified wall-hanging works, most of which did not rely on symmetry or diptych and triptych forms. *Blue Jay Spirit Helper,* 1997 (plate 84), is a freestanding work that is now part of the collection of the University of Alaska, Fairbanks. A female figure is being transformed into a blue jay. The *inua* of the blue jay is represented by faces on each of the bird's wings.

Looner Eclipse, 1999 (plate 94), is a departure from Hoover's earlier work. A quarter moon forms an arc on which five loons rest. The loons are different heights and face in various directions. Layering of the images suggests a sense of depth and space rarely used by Hoover in his carvings.

In 1999, shortly after his eightieth birthday, Hoover underwent triple bypass heart surgery.

> I was never sick until I was eighty years old. I was lucky there; that was quite an achievement. Once I got to be eighty, I aged eighty years—had triple bypass surgery and spent two weeks in the hospital. I didn't know if I was going to live or die. That was really tough.

Now recovered, Hoover continues to be driven by his need to create:

> The creation of images has become a very serious and important part of my life. A religious aspect has crept slowly to the fore. A closer contact with and a deeper understanding of shamanism, a deeper search within my own consciousness, being more aware of Nature—all of these things are part of the search for fulfillment, which eventually are resolved in my art form and style.[34]

The first carving Hoover completed after his bypass surgery is *Shaman's Journey,* 2000 (plate 62). The sculpture is a circular cutout featuring the face of a shaman, which is illustrated by only the eyes, nose, and mouth. The cheeks of the

Fig. 43. *John and Mary Hoover on Mary's boat Myruda, 1980*

shaman and the outline of the shaman's face have been cut out, a use of positive and negative space not often seen in Hoover's earlier work. The shaman is female and the circle framing her face is made up of ravens, who are escorting the shaman on her journey. Hoover said this sculpture was an important piece not just because of the subject matter, but also because it represented a return to his work as an artist, something he missed during his illness. "I couldn't do anything for months," Hoover lamented. "I lost fifty pounds. I didn't know whether I was dead or alive. It was good to start carving again."

Since his illness, Hoover's works are more roughly carved, with broader gouges in the wood. The wood is thicker, with less carved away from the original cedar plank. In most of his diptychs and triptychs, he is no longer carving the backs of the pieces. He is still working large, creating many freestanding works, mobiles, and wall-hangings. He continues to experiment with singular pieces that do not involve hinging, such as *Salmon Woman*, 2000 (plate 103), *Salmon Woman Transforming Into Her Puffin Spirit Helper,* 2000 (plate 105), and *Woman Shaman Transforming Into Her Eagle Spirit Helper,* 2000 (plate 106). He has also expanded his triptych forms, with a new interest in the totem form. He is creating what he calls "triple triptychs," with a repetition of the triptych form and images stacked in threes, such as in *Aleut Totem,* 2000 (plate 100).

Hoover's most recent idea for an artwork, yet to be realized, is to create a fifteen-foot-high fountain cast in bronze: "It'll have a base of rocks and I'll put beads that look like salmon eggs...a salmon woman and the salmon, coming back to spawn with her." Water will run down the figures. The fish will be made out of sheet copper and "they'll be bent and twisted so that, when the water hits them, they'll move and animate it."

Looking back on his artistic career, Hoover said, "I'm very proud of it, I guess.

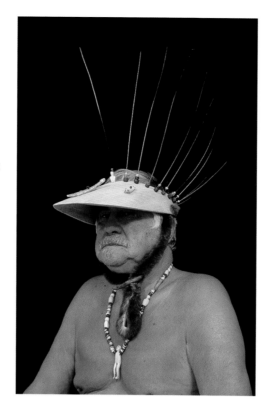

Fig. 44. *John Hoover in Aleut hunting hat, 1999.*

Grateful that [my work] was accepted; that people bought it. I have very few pieces left. I've been doing this for twenty-five years and have maybe a dozen pieces around here [his own home]." Hoover wants people to remember this about him: "That I was a good person with a good sense of humor. That's been an achievement. You can't live without a sense of humor; you've got to laugh once in a while. And music. I love music."

Hoover has also had a second chance at family. In 1985, when Hoover was sixty-five, he and wife Mary welcomed a daughter, Anna, into the world.

I remember Mary was concerned with my age and asked the doctor if it would affect the baby. The doctor said the baby would probably be smart and left-handed. Anna is left-handed and a straight-A student. We have been together every day for almost sixteen years. Anna and Mary have kept me young and happy. Together we have given slide presentations of my artwork at the Heard Museum and at the Frank Lloyd Wright Auditorium at Taliesin West. Since I'm hard of hearing, Anna would field and answer questions and explain the slides as they were projected. After the presentations, everyone came and talked to Anna! She took nine orders for art commissions that day (fig. 45).

They continue to make their home in Grapeview. In his eighty-first year, John Hoover continues to be an inspiration, not just for those who dedicate their lifetimes to creating art, mastering their craft, breaking new ground, and reviving ancient cultures, but also for those who want to live life it to its fullest and richest potential. Hoover's work tells of ancient spirits and ancient peoples, but hidden among the tales is a much more personal story—the story of one man who has spent a lifetime creating. Hoover is an Aleut and a modern man who has forged a unique path through his life, as an artist and a fisherman, a musician and a storyteller. In each of these roles, he has striven to dedication, perseverance, and perfection.

FINAL THOUGHTS

Hoover has made a unique contribution to the realms of contemporary Alaskan art and contemporary Native art. Interest in Native traditions has grown in the last fifty years and has produced a renaissance of lost arts throughout Alaska and the Northwest. The revival of traditional arts among Pacific Northwest Coast Indians, Athabaskans, and Inupiats is reflected in many major works of art. The preservation of tradition, and artistic revival, has been a powerful means of strengthening Native identity and sense of community.[35] Many, like Hoover, have worked to reclaim that heritage and to discover the ancient traditions that have been lost.

A major revival of Northwest Coast art began in the 1950s. Artists working within the highly formalized traditional conventions needed to understand the entire cultural complex, both as a resource for their art and to give it context. The art revival inspired an overall cultural revival, as myths, songs, dances, ceremonies, and histories were rediscovered by artists and passed along. While earlier generations of Native artists had, as expected, worked with traditional compositions, contemporary artists like Hoover view Native traditions as an inspiration and theme. They have redefined the rules to permit extensive borrowing, adaptation, and innovation; artists not only research and develop artistic styles and images of their own cultural heritage, but work outside of their personal affiliations as well.

Hoover aligns himself with other prominent Native artists whom he sees as innovators, such as Charles Loloma, Fritz Scholder, and T. C. Cannon. He knew Loloma and Scholder particularly well, but appreciated Cannon primarily through his artwork. Loloma (1921–1991) was a Hopi who, after years of working with clay and weaving, began making jewelry. He was a self-taught silversmith and his earliest metal works were mainly cast objects designed in a traditional Hopi fashion. From 1962 until 1965 he taught at the Institute of American Indian Arts in Santa Fe. Loloma was known for including "inner gems" in his jewelry. These stones, hidden on the inner side of his jewelry pieces, were meant to indicate the inner beauty of the wearer.

Fritz Scholder (b. 1937) was born in Minnesota and grew up in North Dakota, South Dakota, and Wisconsin. He was one-quarter Luisen, a California Mission tribe. In 1957 Scholder moved with his family to Sacramento, California, where he studied art with Wayne Thiebaud. Scholder joined Thiebaud, along with Grey Kondos and Peter Vandenberg, in creating a cooperative gallery in Sacramento. Scholder later studied art at the University of Arizona in Tuscon and received an M.F.A. degree there. In 1964 he accepted the position of instructor of advanced painting and contemporary art history at the newly formed Institute of American Indian Arts in Santa Fe. There he created a series of paintings depicting what he called the "real Indian." The series was controversial, as Scholder was the first to paint Indians with American flags and beer cans, targeting national clichés. Scholder resigned from the Institute in 1969 and traveled to Europe and Africa. He eventually returned to Santa

Fig. 45. *John Hoover and daughter Anna, 1994.*

Fe, where he built a house and studio. In the 1970s he began making lithographs and became widely known for that medium. In 1972 Scholder was invited by the National Museum of American Art of the Smithsonian Institution to have a two-person show of his own work and that of one of his former students at the Institute. Scholder chose T. C. Cannon and the exhibition received good reviews and traveled to Romania, Yugoslavia, Berlin, and London. He has since been featured in many books, monographs, and a PBS documentary. Scholder was interested in the ways in which humans relate to one another, the land, technology, and history. Like Hoover, he did not grow up as an Indian—this gave the two artists a similarity of experience, but a unique experience to bring to the art world at large. Both Scholder and Hoover were exploring their own identities in relation their own ancestors' heritage and other ancient cultures.

T. C. Cannon (1946–1978), a Native American of Kiowa-Caddo ancestry, was born in Lawton, Oklahoma. By the time Cannon was sixteen years old, he was studying at the Institute of American Indian Arts in Santa Fe where he was introduced to Scholder. After two years of study at the Institute in Santa Fe, he left for one year to study at the San Francisco Art Institute. In 1969 Cannon returned to Santa Fe for another year to study philosophy and painting. In 1971 he entered Central State University in Edmond, Oklahoma, where he graduated three years later. In 1974 he again returned to Santa Fe to make it his permanent home, but he was soon invited to spend one year as an artist-in-residence at Dartmouth College. During this year in Hanover, New Hampshire, he developed a collaborative relationship with Japanese master woodcarver Maeda and master printer Uchikawa, who were also working as artists-in-residence. The friendship between the three artists continued until the time of Cannon's death. This resulted in the highly acclaimed publication of the

Memorial Woodcut Suite. Cannon was only thirty-three when he died in an automobile accident in Santa Fe.

All of these artists helped to revise and replace outmoded and paternalistic concepts of Native crafts with a new and vigorous category of "art by artists who happen to be Indian." They, along with Hoover, accepted the challenge to interpret their culture in ways that combine innovation and tradition. They were also willing to explore techniques and materials that were non-Native, drawing on images and methods from Europe, Asia, and Africa. Through the efforts of these and other artists, Native art has continued to flourish both in its original cultural context and in the international art world.

A new generation of artists, younger than Hoover, who have apprenticed with established master artists is now beginning to emerge. The best of these artists have been able to balance tradition with the need to innovate and to represent modern issues. The number of female artists in Northwest Coast and Alaskan art has also been growing, which has increased the awareness and appreciation of traditional materials and techniques such as weaving and appliqué, as well as the woodcarvings done by many female artists. Women have taken these traditional forms and turned them into truly original and innovative contemporary work. New materials such as glass, bronze, mixed media, and fabricated materials have also been introduced, though many artists still continue to work in such traditional materials as gold, silver, argillite, wood, and graphics. Native artists have also taken their work into public places, with many large-scale site-specific installations.

Hoover has contributed to the renaissance and revival of the lost arts. He found himself among others who were doing the same, although his artistic and personal motivations came almost solely from within. He has preserved ancient stories from cultures such as that of the Aleuts, which had almost been lost. From ancient materials and methods, Hoover has borrowed, adapted, and innovated, taking traditional tools, templates, and designs and transforming them into his own creations. Through his innovation, he has defined what it is to be an artist and what it is to be a Native American artist. He has strengthened Native identity, exhibiting his works in museums and galleries throughout the world. His dedication to his art and his craft is an inspiration for young generations now emerging and generations yet to come.

Hoover calls his work "an obsession, something I have to do. If I'm not doing it I don't feel whole. Sometimes I struggle, but it has got to come. Creating something makes you feel joyous, especially in the moment you are doing it."[36]

The rest of us are fortunate for his obsession.

Notes

1. Unless otherwise attributed, all quotes by John Hoover in this text are from an interview conducted by the author in Grapeview, Washington, in January 2000.

2. Fitzhugh, William W., and Aron Crowell. *Crossroads of Continents: Cultures of Siberia and Alaska* (Washington, D.C.: Smithsonian Institution Press, 1988) 326.

3. Duane Niatum, personal interview, 1996.

4. Katz, Jane B. *This Song Remembers: Self-Portraits of Native Americans in the Arts* (Boston: Houghton Mifflin, 1980) 34.

5. Niatum, personal interview, 1996.

6. Katz 1980, 34.

7. Artist statement from Hoover's 1978 exhibition at the Haines Gallery, Seattle, Washington.

8. Niatum, personal interview, 1996.

9. Dixon-Kennedy. *Native American Myth and Legend* (London: Blanford, 1996) 124.

10. Niatum, Duane. "Shamanism, Sacred Narratives, the Sea, and Cedar in the Art of John Hoover, Aleut Sculptor" (University of Michigan Ph.D. dissertation 0127, 1997) 153.

11. Niatum 1997, 52.

12. Niatum 1997, 64.

13. Niatum 1997, 63

14. Stewart, Hilary. *Cedar* (Seattle: University of Washington Press, 1994) 22.

15. Niatum, personal interview, 1996.

16. Dunham, Mike. "Linked by Heritage: Two Artists with Roots in Alaska Find Fame in What Makes Them Different." *Anchorage Daily News* (27 Nov 1994) K3.

17. Holm, Bill. *Northwest Coast Indian Art: An Analysis of Form* (Seattle: University of Washington Press, 1965) 35.

18. Ames, Kenneth M., and Herbert D.G. Mascher. *People of the Northwest Coast: Their Archaeology and Prehistory* (London: Thames & Hudson, 1999) 223.

19. Niatum 1997, 170.

20. Holm 1965, 26.

21. Shearar, Cheryl. *Understanding Northwest Coast Art: A Guide to Crests, Beings and Symbols* (Seattle: University of Washington Press, 2000) 50.

22. Shearar 2000, 44.

23. Shearar 2000, 85.

24. Monathan, Doris, and Guy Monathan. "John Hoover." *Journal of American Indian Art.* (Winter 1978).

25. Katz 1980, 34.

26. Shearar 2000, 79.

27. Fitzhugh and Crowell 1988, 56.

28. Niatum 1997, 40-41.

29 Niatum 1997, 85.

30. Black, Lydia T. *Aleut Art.* (Anchorage: Aang Angain Press, Aleutian / Pribilof Islands Association, 1982) 79.

31. Dunham, Mike. "Art After Alaska: Expatriate Artists...{New lives on Puget Sound}." *Anchorage Daily News* (13 September 1998) K1.

32. Shearar 2000, 64.

33. Shearar 2000, 48.

34. Niatum 1997, 63.

35. Ritter, Harry. *Alaska's History: The People, the Land and Events of the North Country* (Anchorage: Alaska Northwest Books, 1993) 29.

36. Anstine, Dennis. Totem Tidings: "The Sculptor Is a Fisherman or the Fisherman Is a Sculptor." *The Daily Olympian Sunday* (24 Oct 1976).

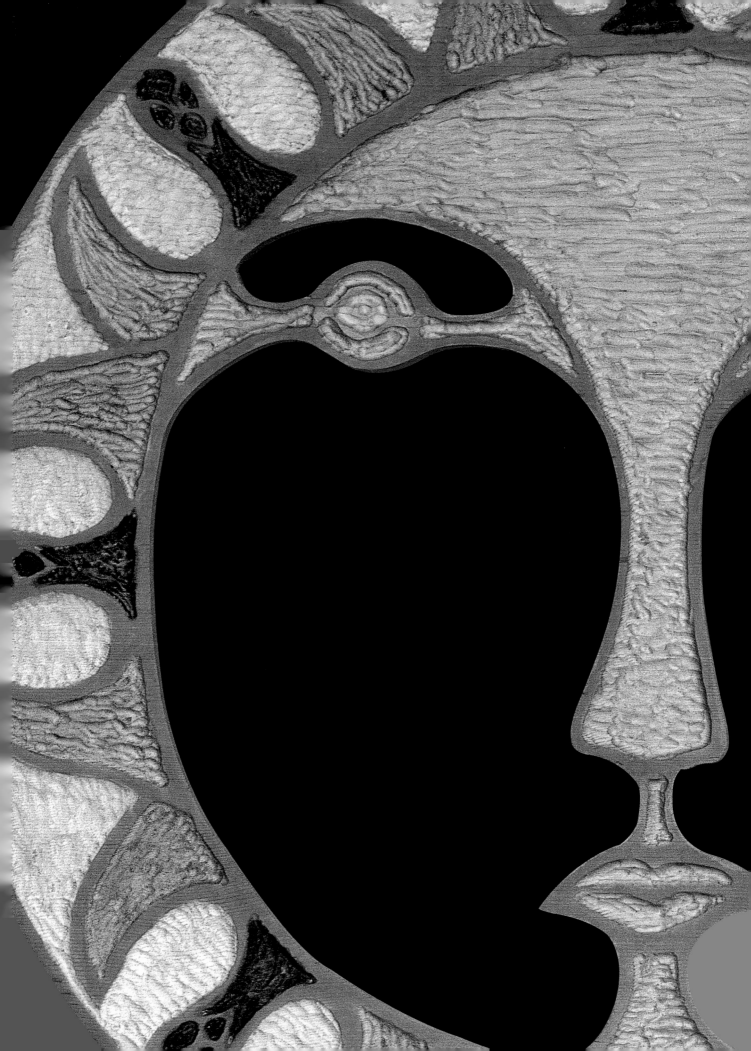

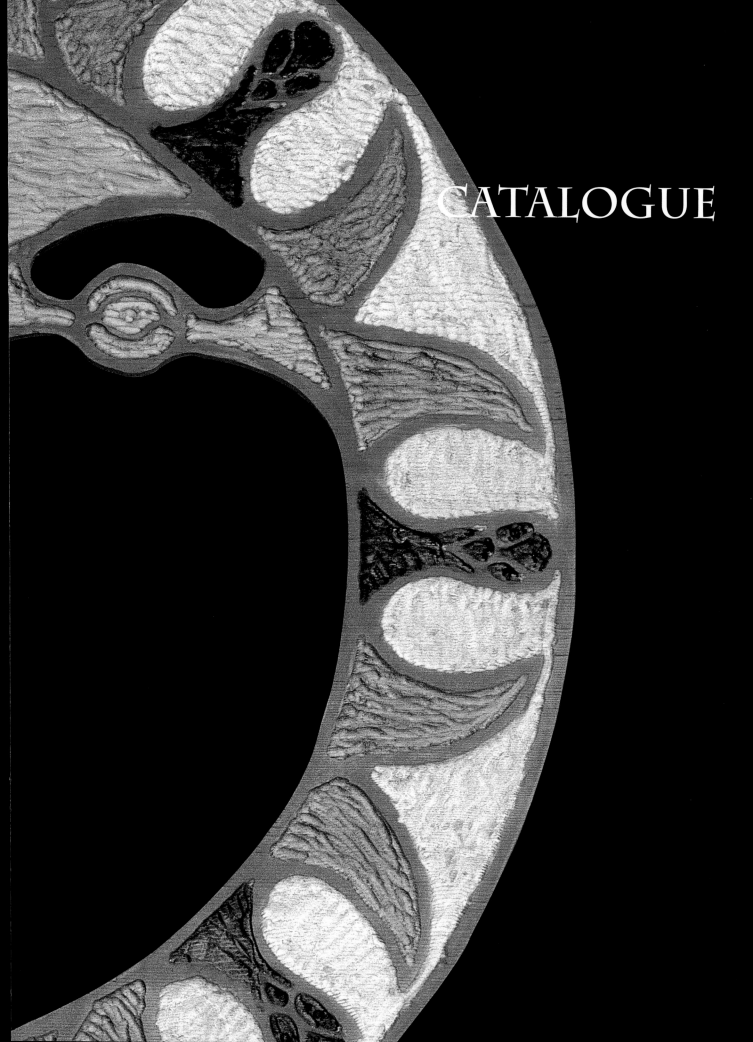

CATALOGUE

PLATE 1
Cannery Row, 1950
Oil on board, 4 x 6 in.

6 8

PLATE 2
Mt. Eccles, Cordova, Alaska, 1950
Oil on board, 6 x 8 in.

PLATE 3
Lake Eyak, Cordova, Alaska, 1950
Oil on board, 8 x 10 in.

PLATE 4
Out My Studio Window, 1956
Oil on board, 18 x 24 in.

PLATE 5
Owl and the Pussy Cat, 1957
Oil on board, 24 x 20 in.

PLATE 6
Self-Portrait, 1957
Oil on board, 30 x 12 in.

PLATE 7
Eyak Church, 1959
Oil on board, 36 x 24 in.

PLATE 8
Fish Camp, 1959
Oil on board, 20 x 24 in.

PLATE 9
Putting Out the Lead, 1960
Oil on board, 18 x 24 in.

76

PLATE 10
Stake Net, 1961
Oil on board, 22 x 30 in.

Plate 11
Maltese Cross Cedar Mill, 1970
Oil on board, 22 x 30 in.

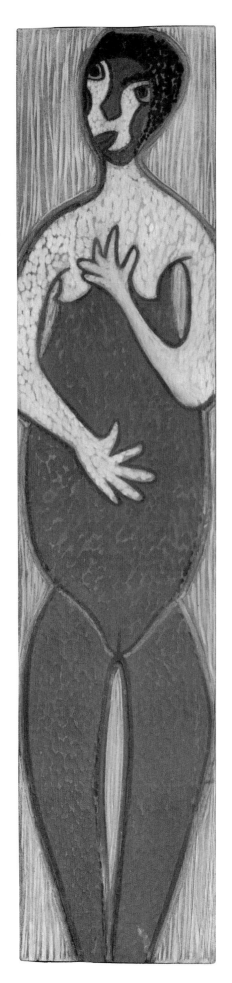
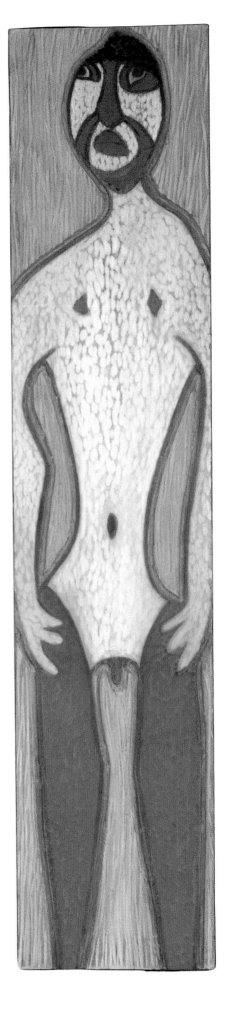

PLATE 12
Adam and Eve, 1967
Cedar, 42 x 9.5 in.

Plate 13
Phoenix Bird, 1968
Cedar, 12 x 32 in.

80

Plate 14
Feast Dish, 1969
Alder, 48 x 12 in.

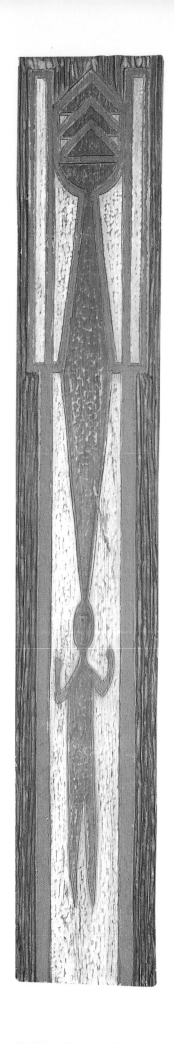

PLATE 15
Spirit Board, 1970
Cedar, 55 x 9 in.

Plate 16
Aleut Ancestor Spirit Board, 1970
Cedar, 60 x 9 in.

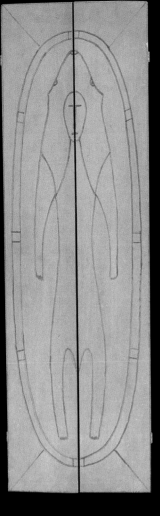

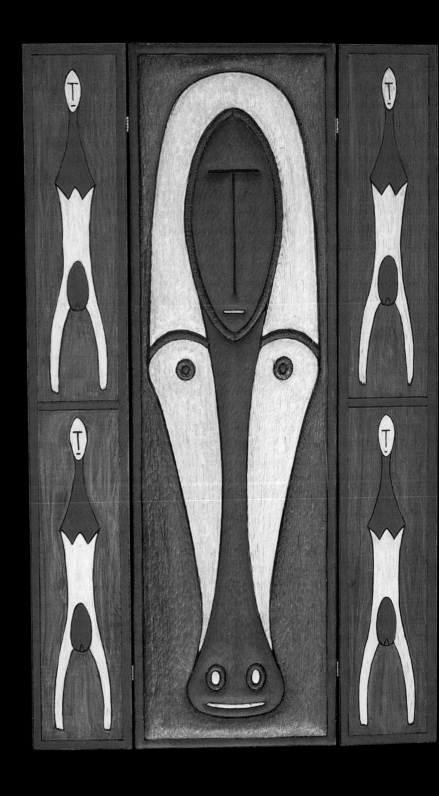

Plate 17
Polar Bear Spirit, 1971
Cedar, 36 x 12 in. (closed)
36 x 24 in. (open)

PLATE 18
Grebe Mask, 1972
Cedar and beads, 24 x 12 in.

Plate 19
Eagle Spirit Mask, 1972
Cedar and ivory, 18 x 12 in.

86

PLATE 20
Puffin Spirit Mask, 1972
Cedar and ivory, 24 x 12 in.

PLATE 21
Salmon Woman, 1972
Cedar, 11 x 7 in.

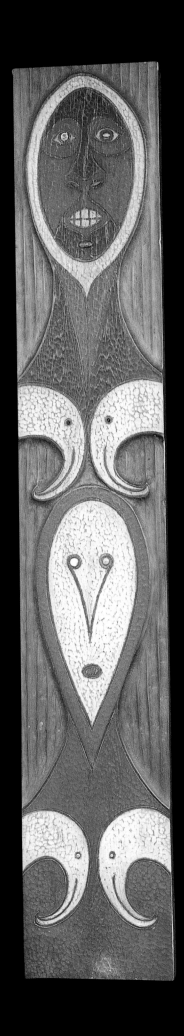

PLATE 22
Raven People, 1972
Cedar and ivory, 72 x 12 in.

Plate 23
Frog Spirit Mask, 1972
Cedar, copper, and ivory, 24 x 20 in.

PLATE 24
Spirit Board, 1973
Cedar, 60 x 9 in.

PLATE 25
Salmon Man, 1974
Cedar, 36 x 24 in.

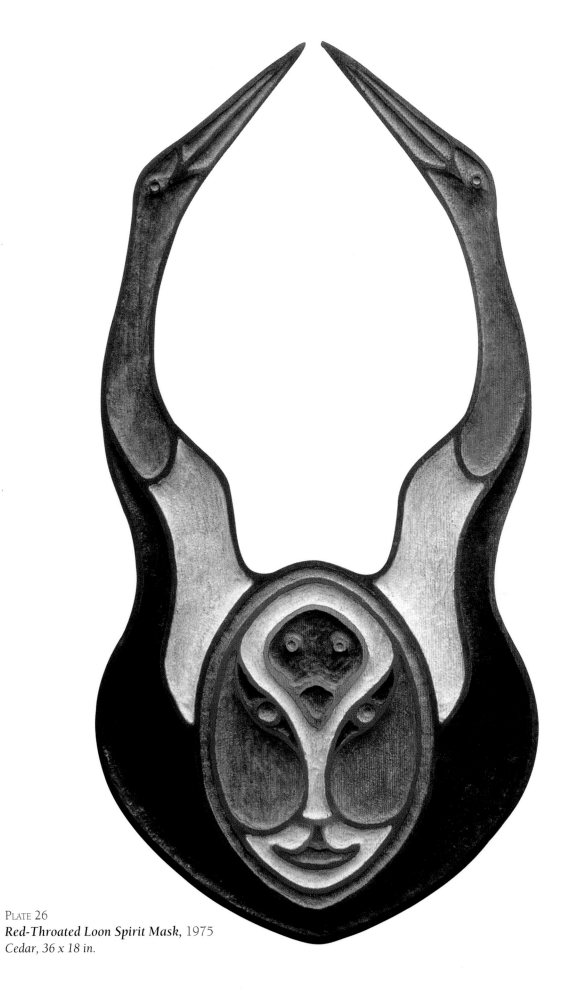

PLATE 26
Red-Throated Loon Spirit Mask, 1975
Cedar, 36 x 18 in.

93

PLATE 27
Whale and Otter Spirit, 1975
Cedar, 36 x 16 in. (closed)

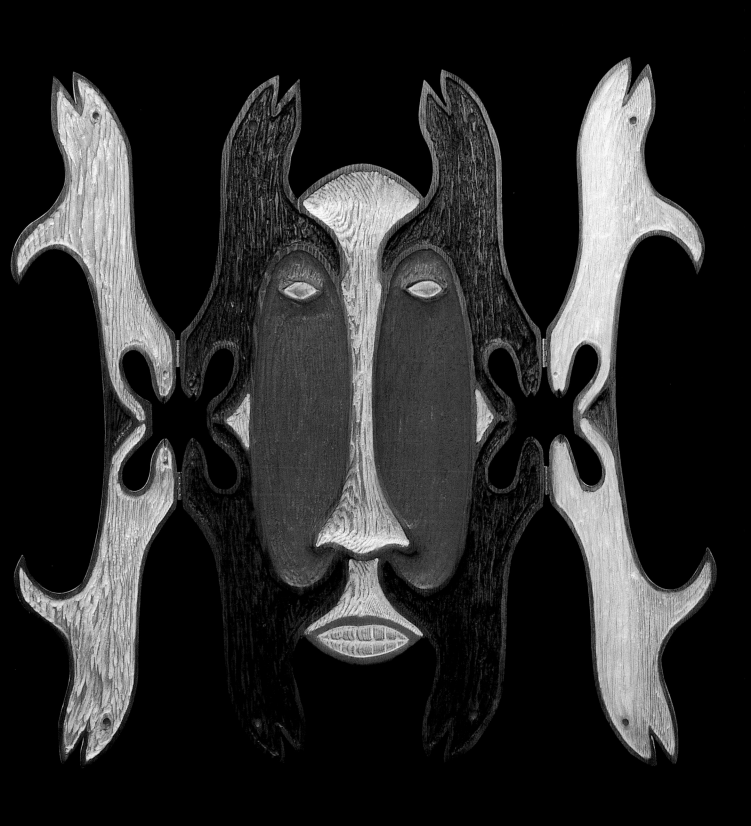

PLATE 28
Whale and Otter Spirit, 1975
Cedar, 36 x 36 in. (open)

PLATE 29
Loon Feast Dish, 1979
Cedar with ivory inlay, 36 x 12 in.

Plate 30
Puffin Spirit, 1980
Cedar, 36 x 36 in.

97

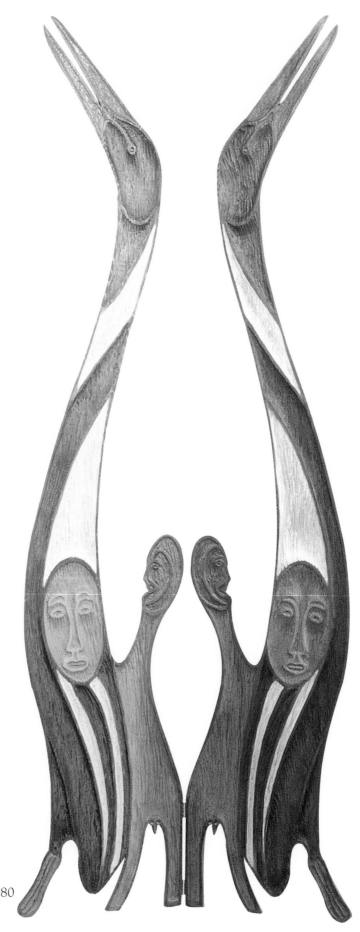

PLATE 31
Blind Man and the Loon, 1980
Cedar, 60 x 24 in.

PLATE 32
Cormorant Spirit Woman, 1980
Cedar, 36 x 24 in.

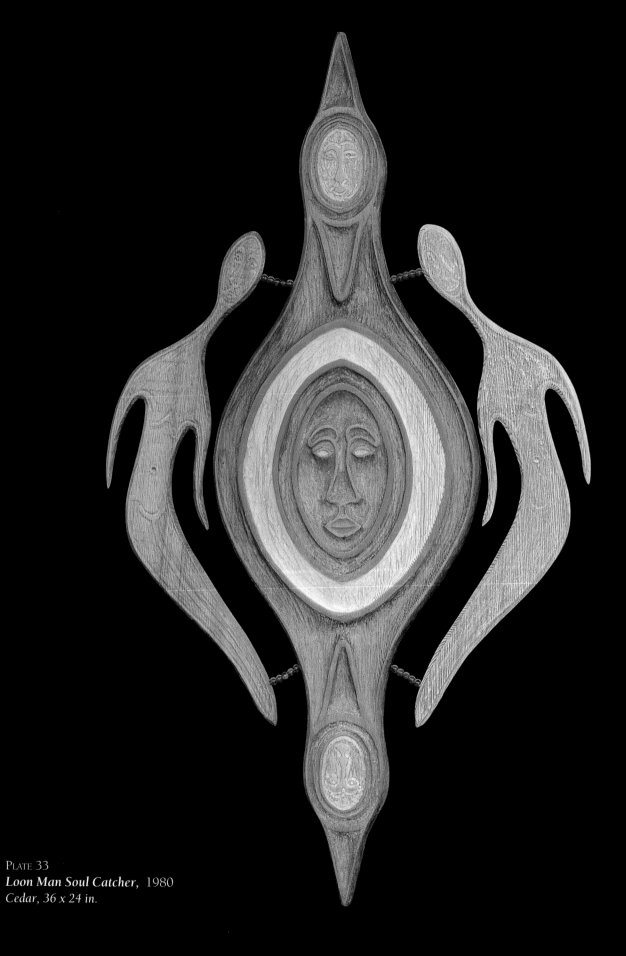

PLATE 33
Loon Man Soul Catcher, 1980
Cedar, 36 x 24 in.

PLATE 34
Loon Woman, 1980
Cedar, 48 x 12 in.

PLATE 35
Octopus Chimes, 1981
Cedar and bronze, 48 x 30 in.

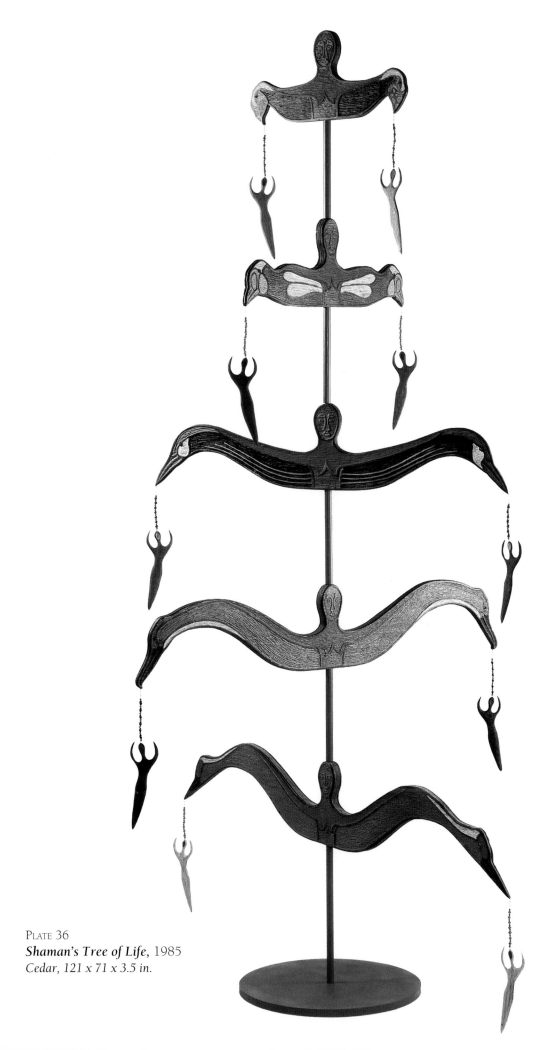

PLATE 36
Shaman's Tree of Life, 1985
Cedar, 121 x 71 x 3.5 in.

PLATE 37
Hummingbird Feeder, 1982
Cedar, 40 x 26 in.

PLATE 38
Salmon People, 1985
Cedar, 48 x 18 in.

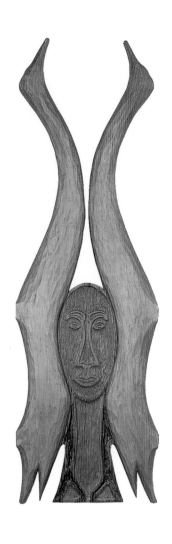

PLATE 39
Grebe Spirit, 1982
Cedar, 48 x 12 in. (closed)
48 x 24 in. (open)

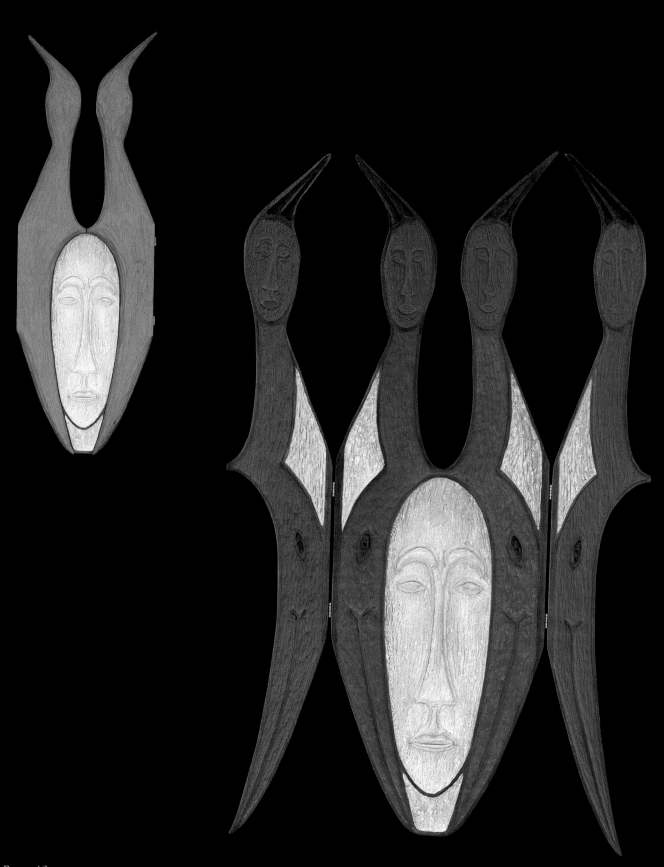

Plate 40
Red-Throated Loon Spirit Mask, 1984
Cedar, 36 x 12 in. (closed)
36 x 24 in. (open)

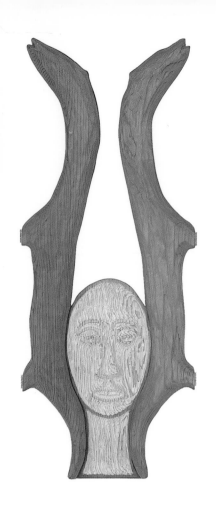

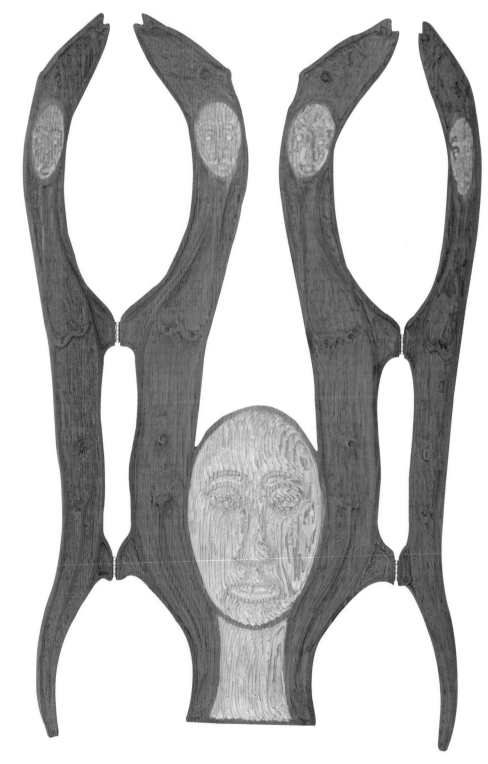

PLATE 41
Dancing Otters, 1985
Cedar, 30 x 9 in. (closed)
30 x 18 in. (open)

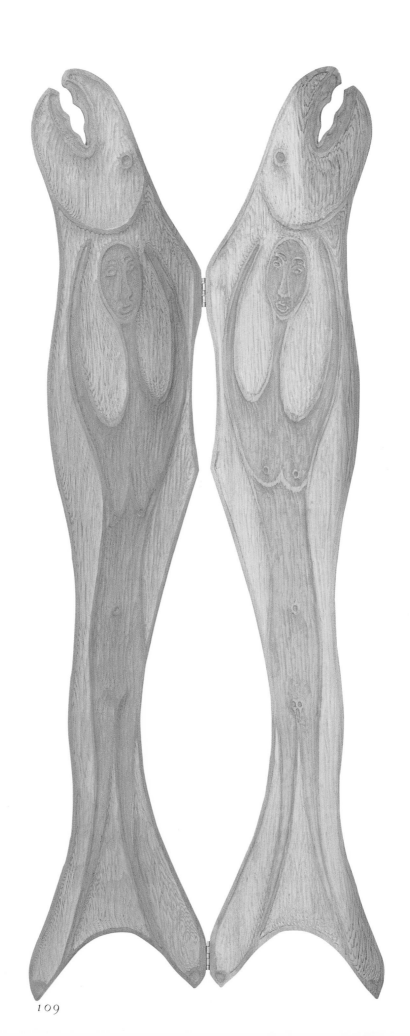

Plate 42
Salmon Women, 1985
Cedar, 48 x 12 in.

109

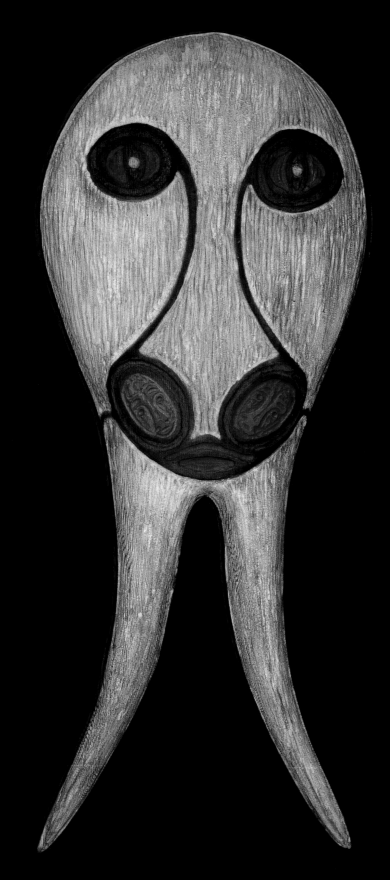

Plate 43
Walrus Spirit Mask, 1985
Cedar, 36 x 12 in.

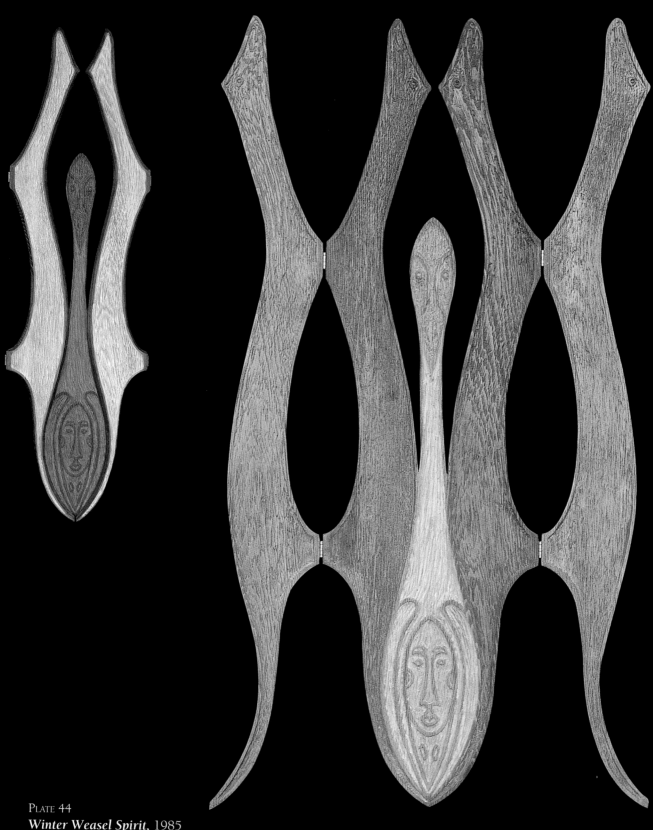

PLATE 44
Winter Weasel Spirit, 1985
Cedar, 36 x 10 in. (closed)
36 x 20 in. (open)

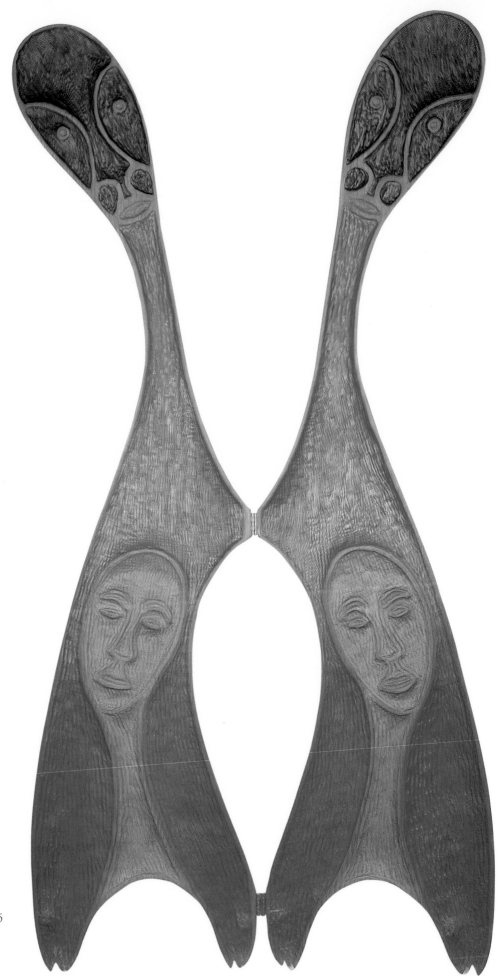

PLATE 45
Seal People, 1985
Cedar, 48 x 24 in.

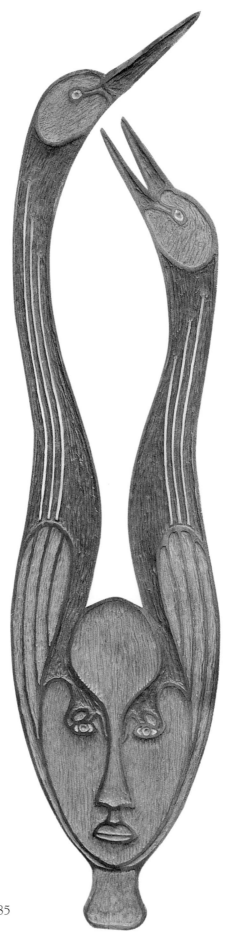

PLATE 46
Underwater Loon Woman, 1985
Cedar, 45 x 11 in.

PLATE 47
Kingfisher Spirit, 1986
Cedar, 18 x 12 in. (closed)
18 x 24 in. (open)

PLATE 48s
Winter Otter Spirit Mask, 1987
Cedar, 24 x 30 in.

PLATE 49
Eagle and Salmon, 1987
Cedar, 48 x 24 in.

PLATE 50
Salmon Man, 1987
Cedar, 36 x 36 in.

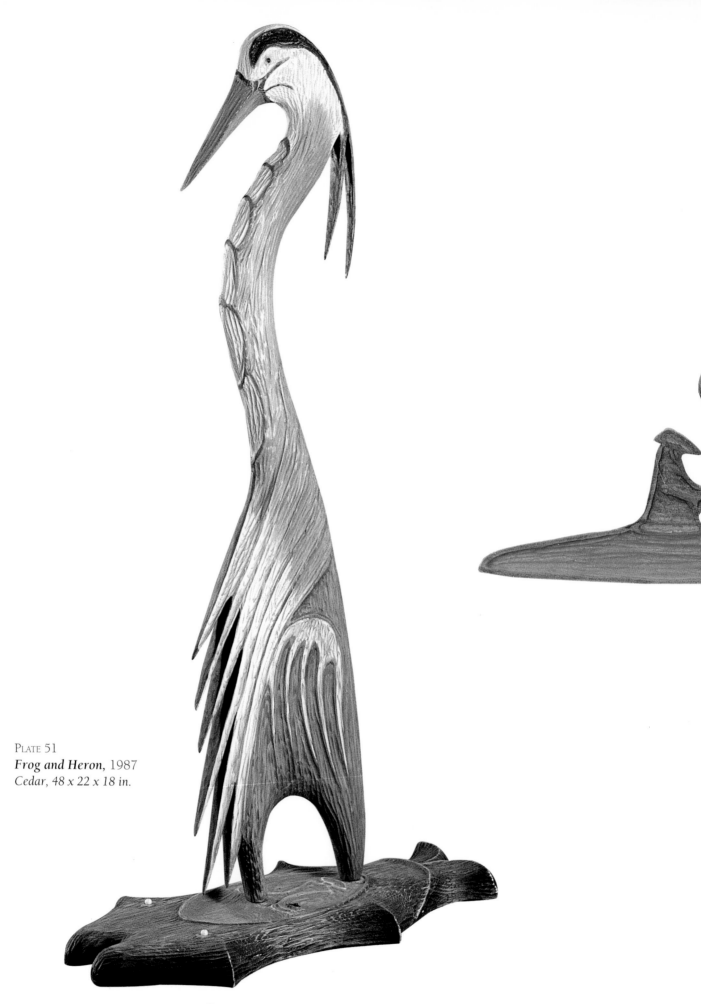

PLATE 51
Frog and Heron, 1987
Cedar, 48 x 22 x 18 in.

PLATE 52
Aleut Hunter Spirit Mask, 1987
Cedar, 22 x 35 in.

1 1 9

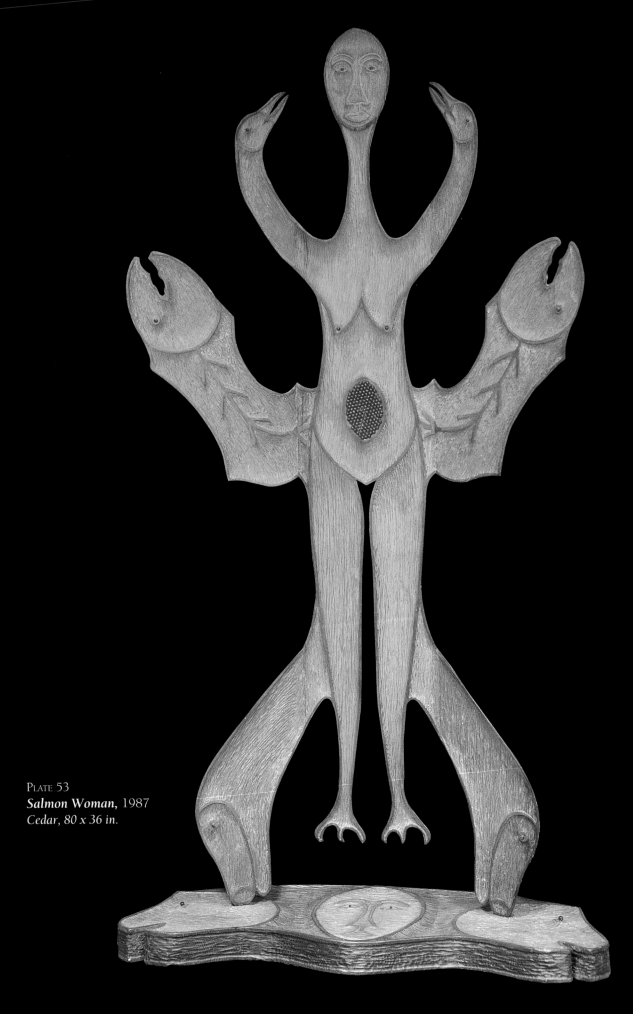

PLATE 53
Salmon Woman, 1987
Cedar, 80 x 36 in.

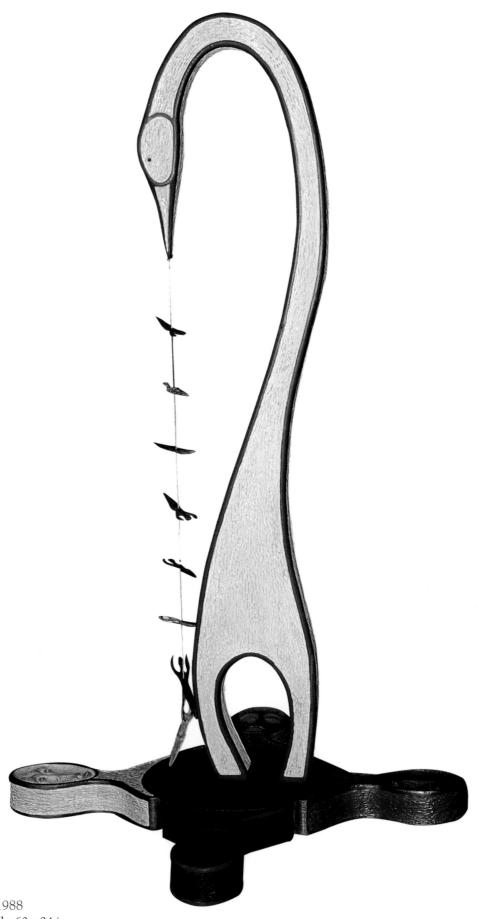

PLATE 54
Swan Spirit, 1988
Cedar and beads, 60 x 24 in.

PLATE 55
Heron People, 1989
Cedar, 48 x 10 in. (closed)
48 x 20 in. (open)

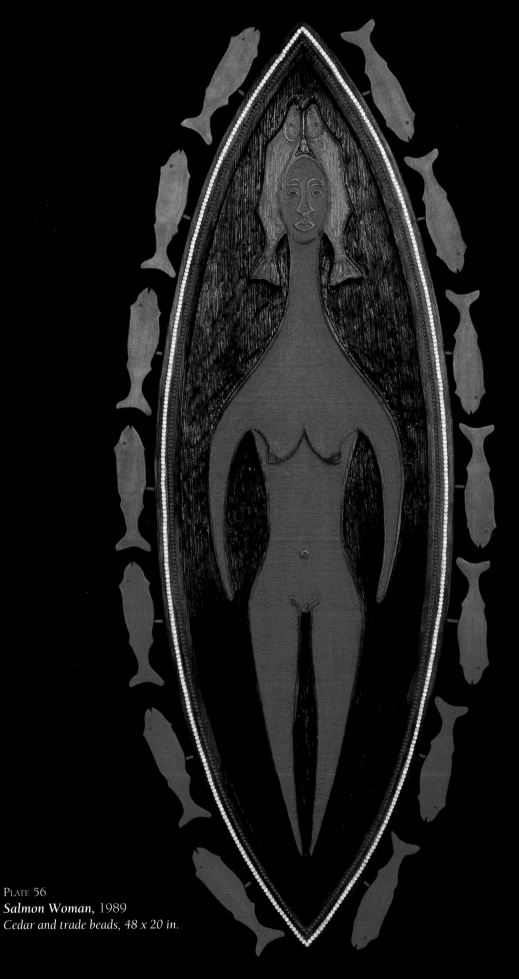

PLATE 56
Salmon Woman, 1989
Cedar and trade beads, 48 x 20 in.

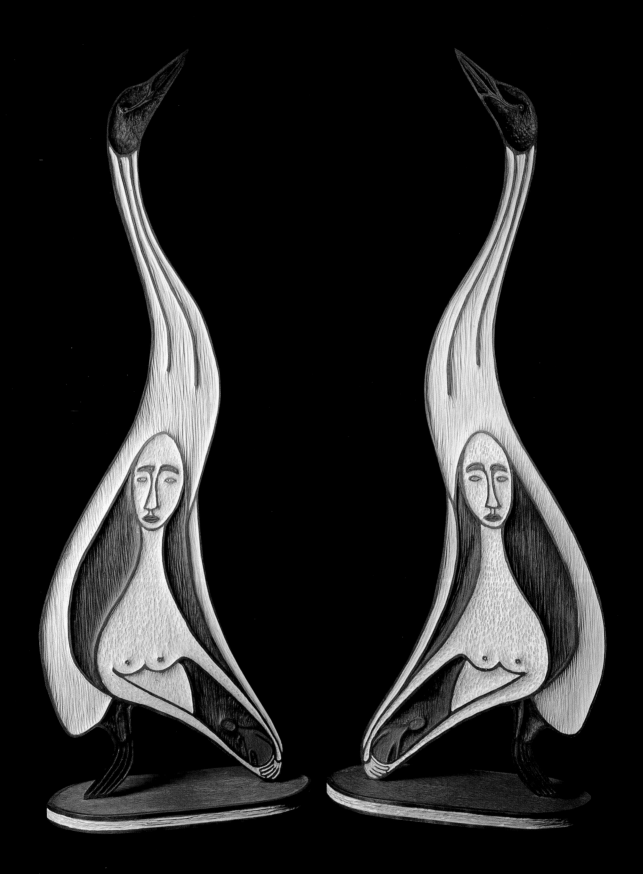

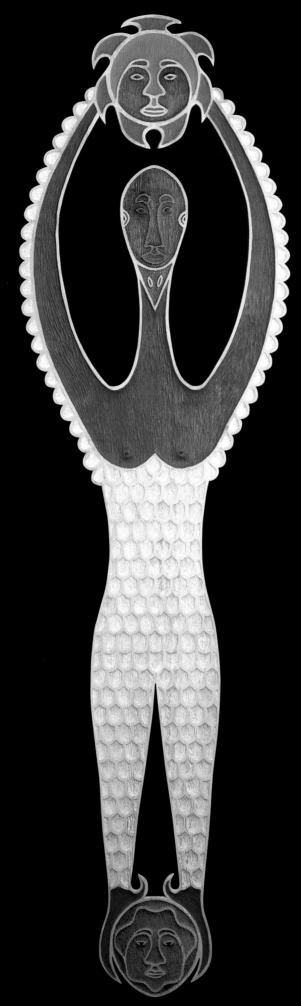

PLATE 58
Raven the Creator, 1989
Cedar, 72 x 30 in.

125

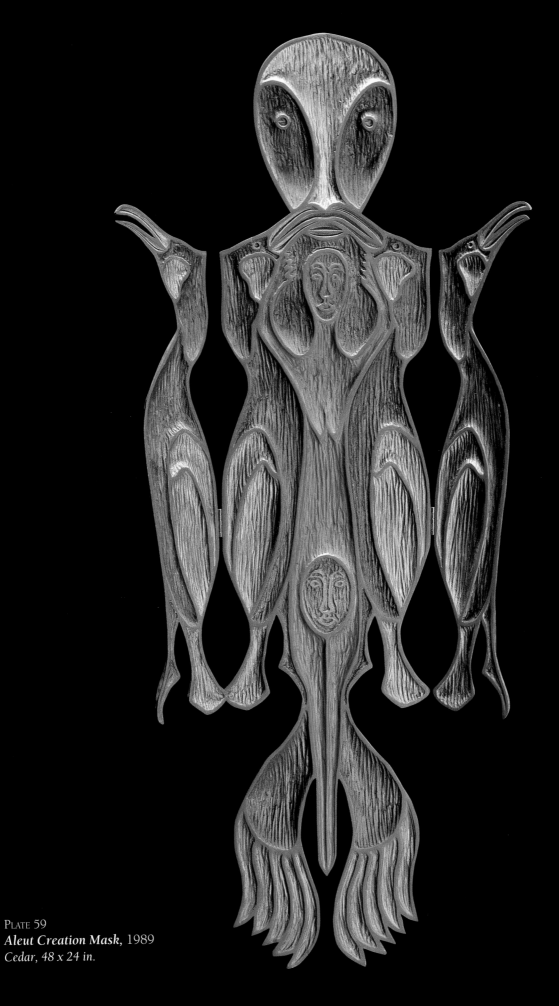

PLATE 59
Aleut Creation Mask, 1989
Cedar, 48 x 24 in.

Plate 60
Seal Spirit Mask, 1989
Cedar, 21 x 11 in.

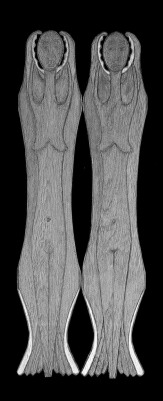

PLATE 61
Salmon Women, 1990
Cedar, 5 x 2 in.

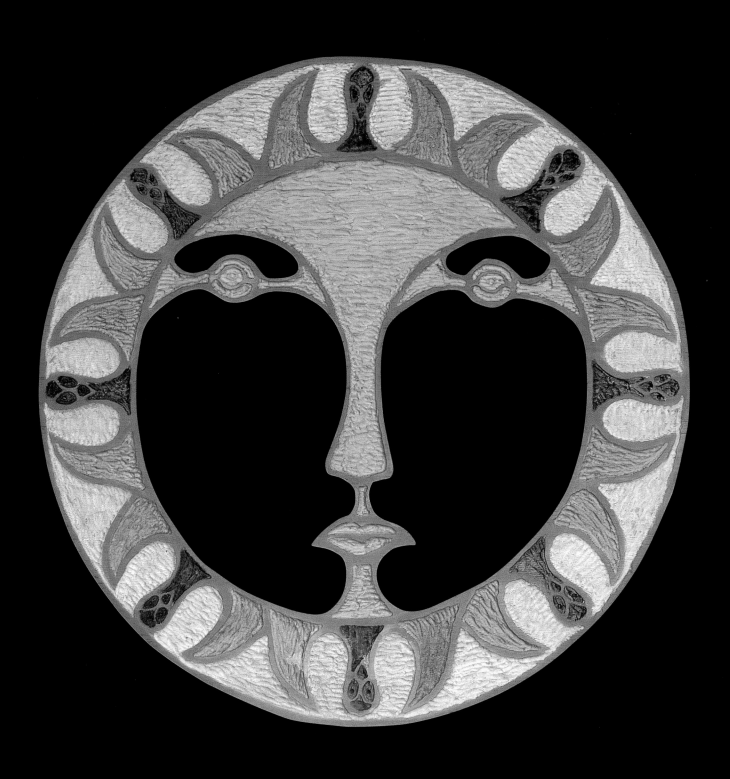

PLATE 62
Shaman's Journey, 2000
Cedar, 32 in. diameter

PLATE 63
Seal Child, 1990
Cedar, 45 x 22 in.

PLATE 64
Walrus Man, 1990
Cedar, 64 x 25 in.

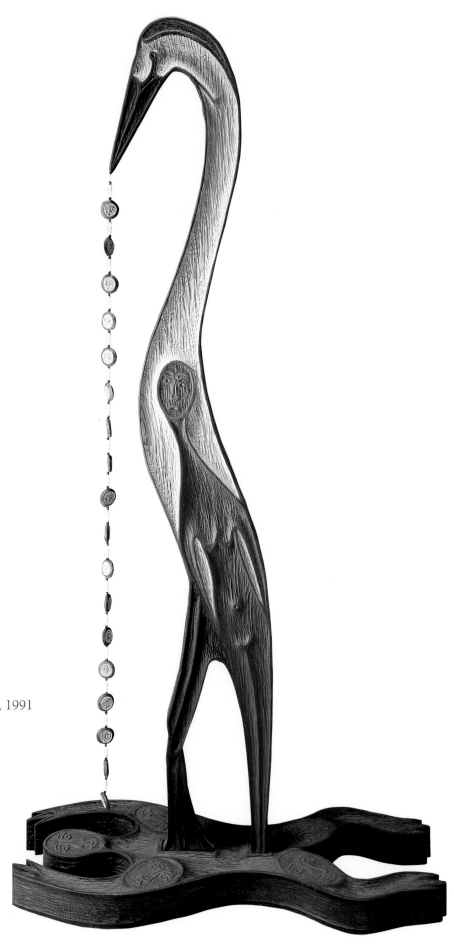

PLATE 65
Heron and Frog Soul Catcher, 1991
Cedar and beads, 72 x 48 in.

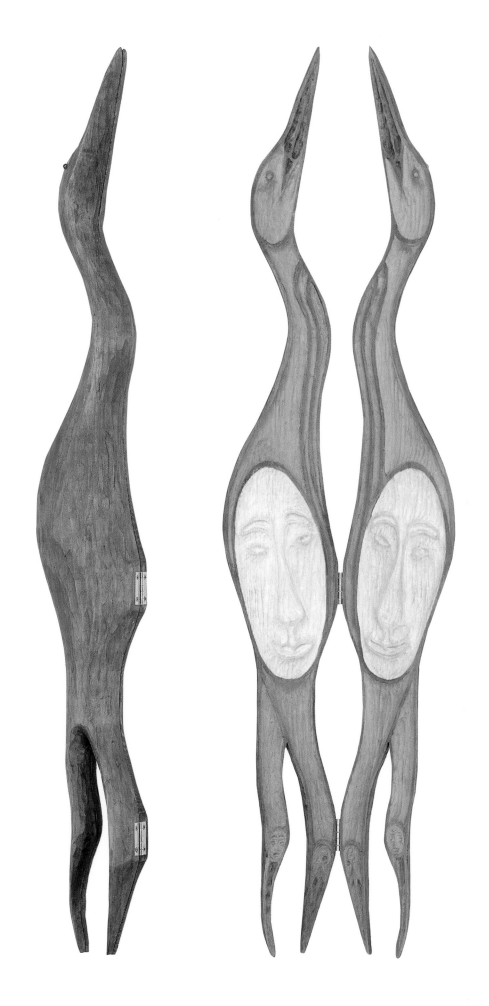

PLATE 66
Loon Spirit, 1991
Cedar, 48 x 6 in. (closed)
48 x 12 in. (open)

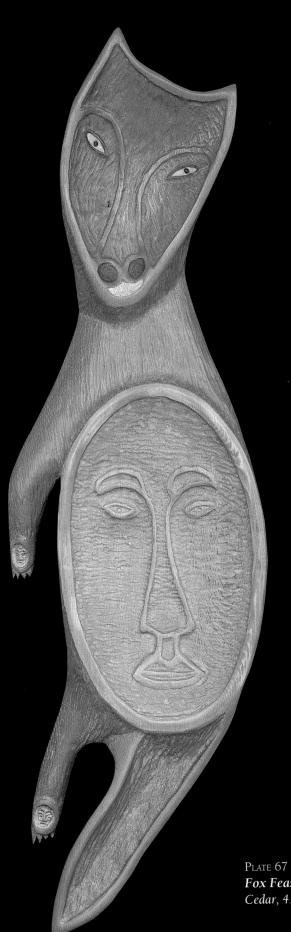

PLATE 67
Fox Feast Dish, 1992
Cedar, 41 x 12 in.

PLATE 68
Aleut Storyboard: Old Man of the Sea, 1993
Cedar, 39 x 73 in.

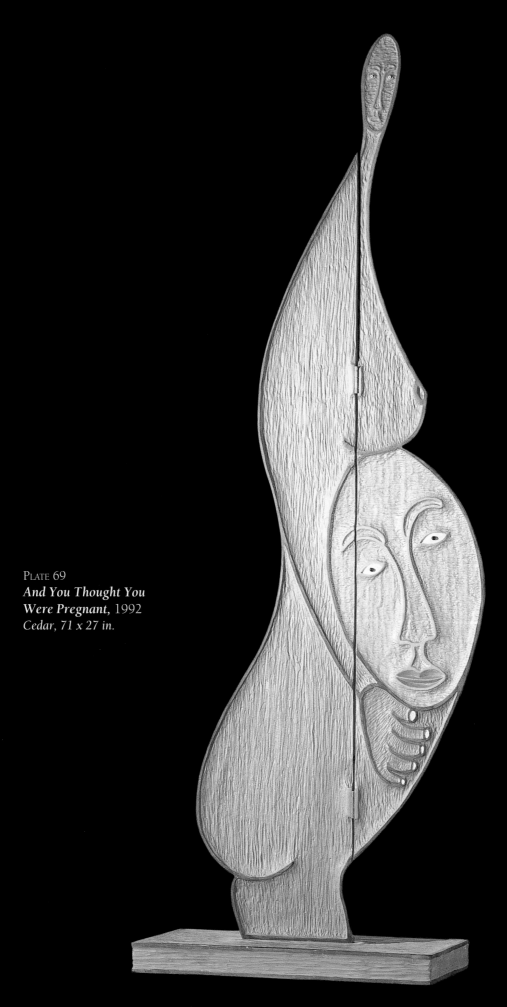

PLATE 69
**And You Thought You
Were Pregnant,** 1992
Cedar, 71 x 27 in.

136

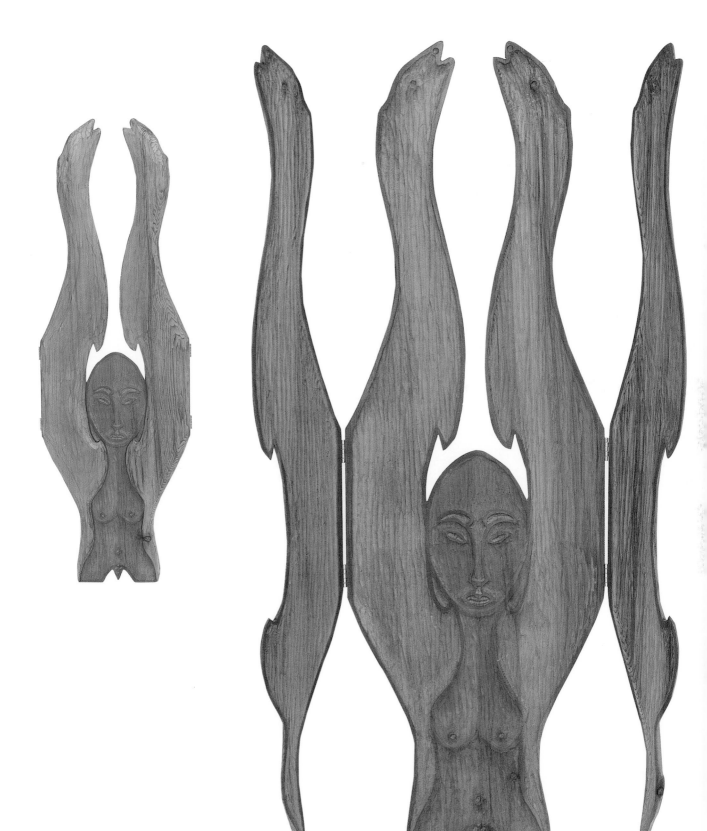

PLATE 70
Otter Spirit, 1992
Cedar, 36 x 12 in. (closed)
36 x 24 in. (open)

Plate 71
Raven the Creator, 1992
Cedar, 48 x 48 in.

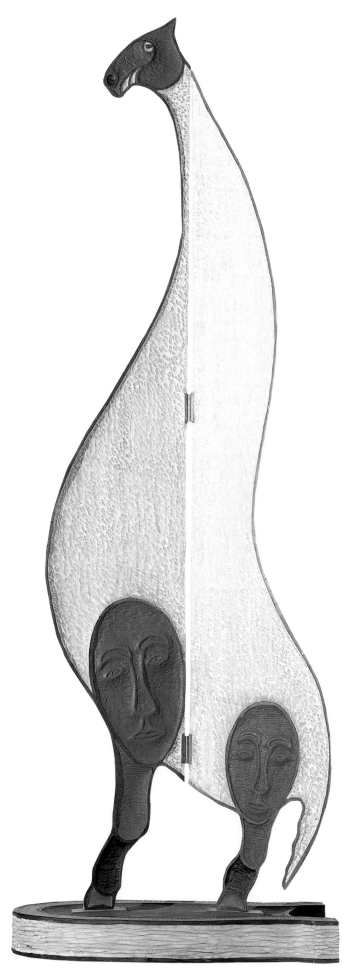

PLATE 72
That's What You Get for Horsing Around, 1993
Cedar, 69 x 24 in.

Plate 73
Loon Spirit, 1993
Cedar, 24 x 9 in. (closed)
24 x 18 in. (open)

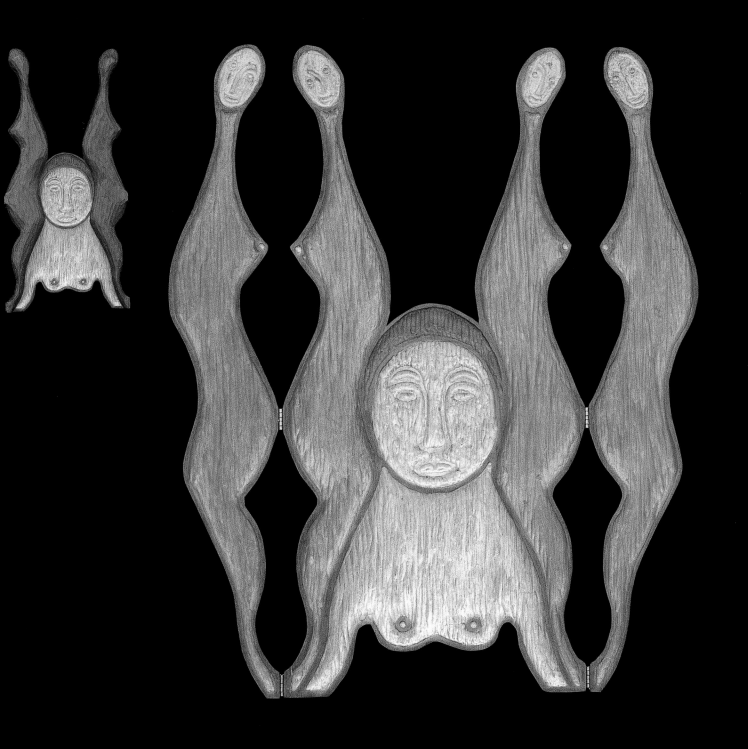

PLATE 74
Baby, 1993
Cedar, 24 x 12 in. (closed)
24 x 18 in. (open)

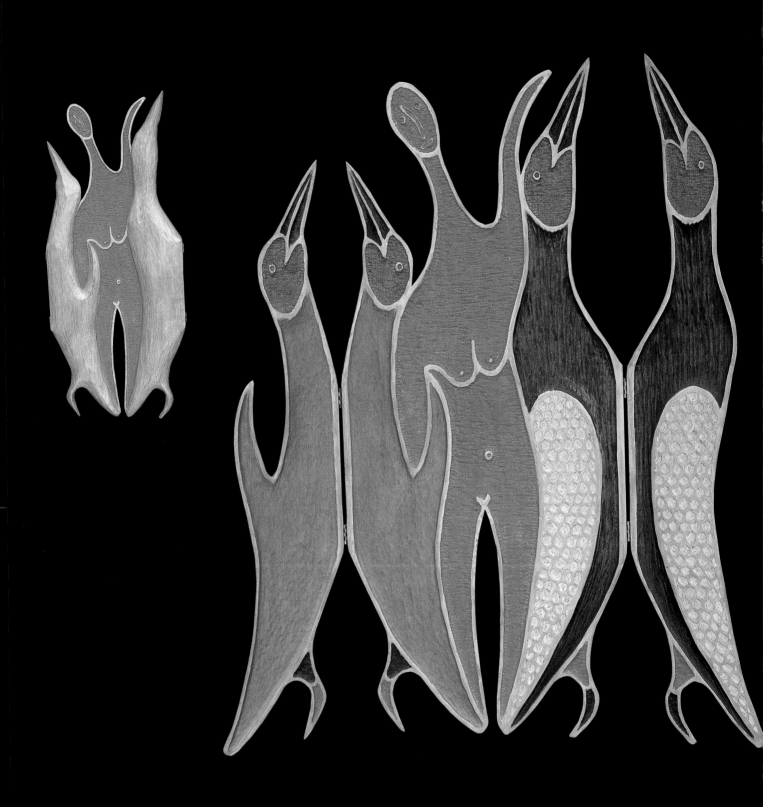

Plate 75
Loon Lady, 1994
Cedar, 34 x 15 in. (closed)
34 x 30 in. (open)

Plate 76
Otter People, 1995
Cedar, 42 x 11 in.

Plate 78
Owl Mask, 1995
Cedar, 36 x 36 in.

Plate 79
Sun, 1995
Cedar, 36 x 36 in.

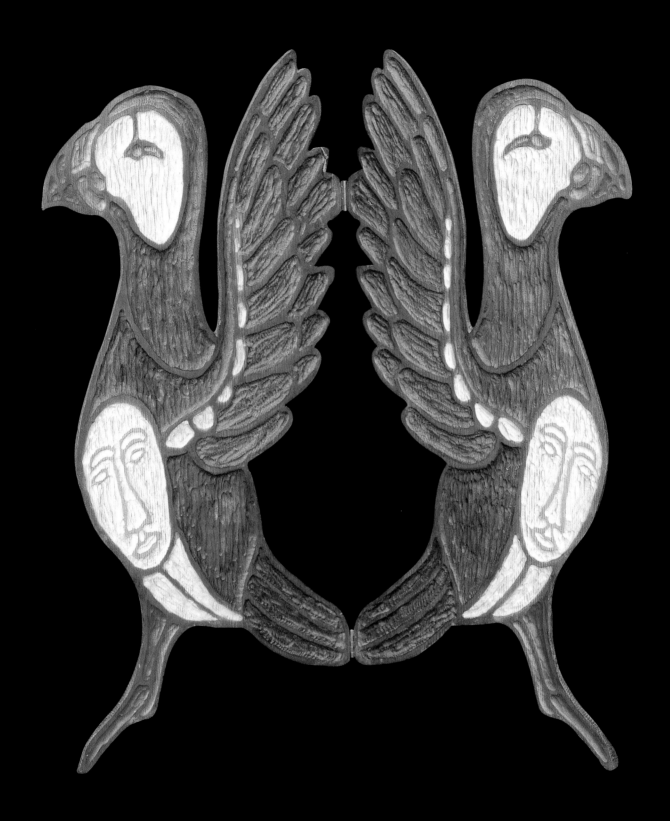

PLATE 80
Puffin, 1996
Cedar and bronze, 24 x 12 in.

Plate 81
Crane Dancers, 1996
Cedar, 60 x 24 in. each

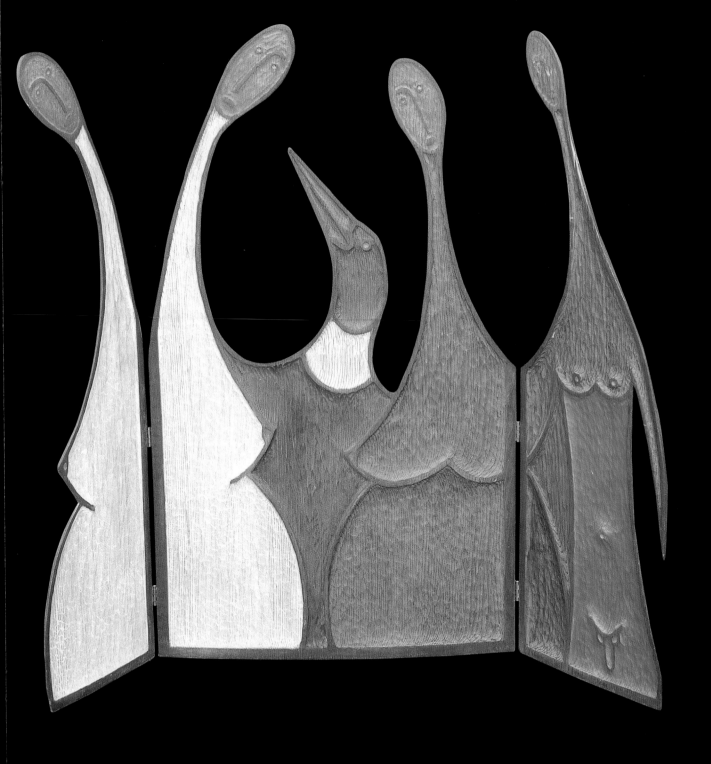

PLATE 82
Loon People, 1996
Cedar and cast aluminum, 18 x 24 in.

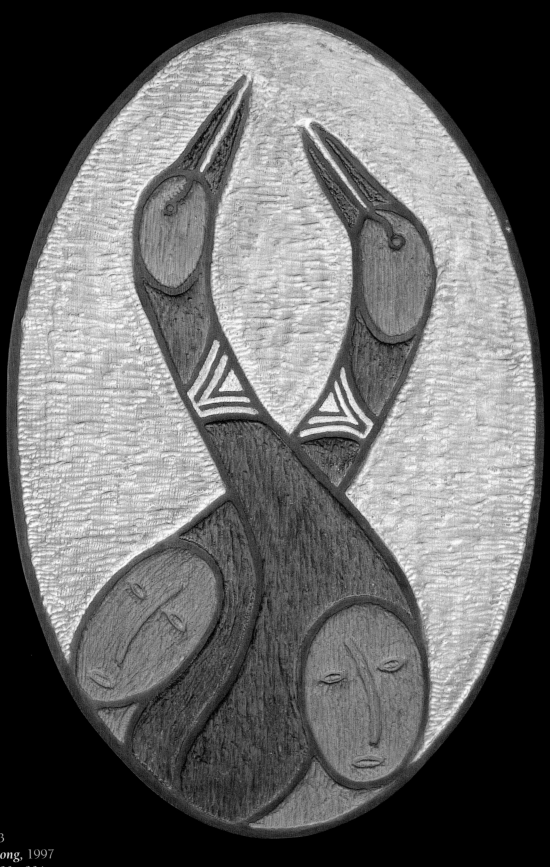

Plate 83
Loon Song, 1997
Cedar, 30 x 20 in.

PLATE 84
Blue Jay Spirit Helper, 1997
Cedar, 75 x 32 in.

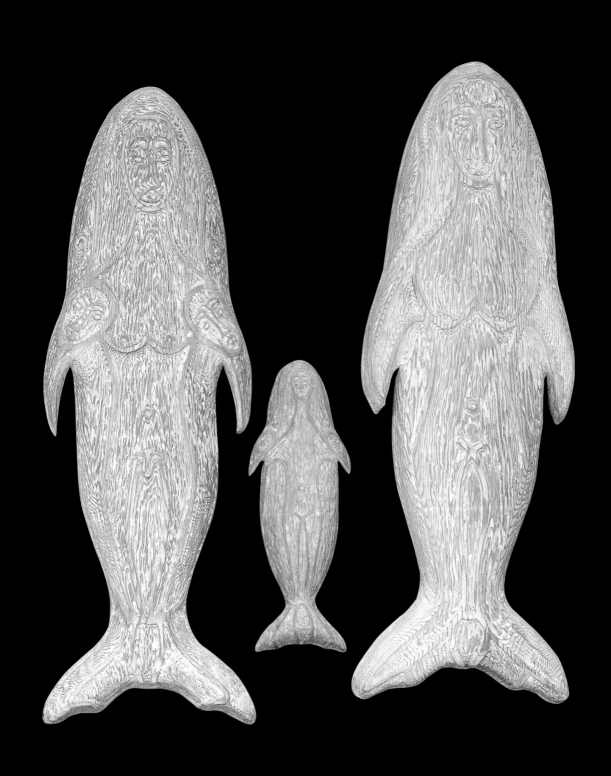

PLATE 85
Whale Family, 1997
Cedar, large: 32 x 12 in., small: 15 x 6 in.

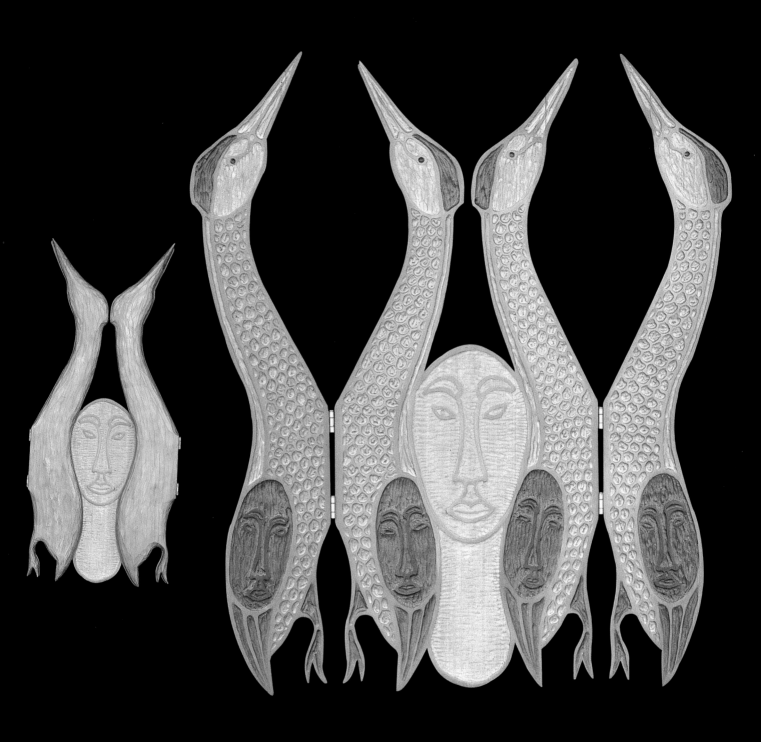

PLATE 86
Red-Throated Grebe, 1995
Cedar, 30 x 13 in. (closed)
30 x 24 in. (open)

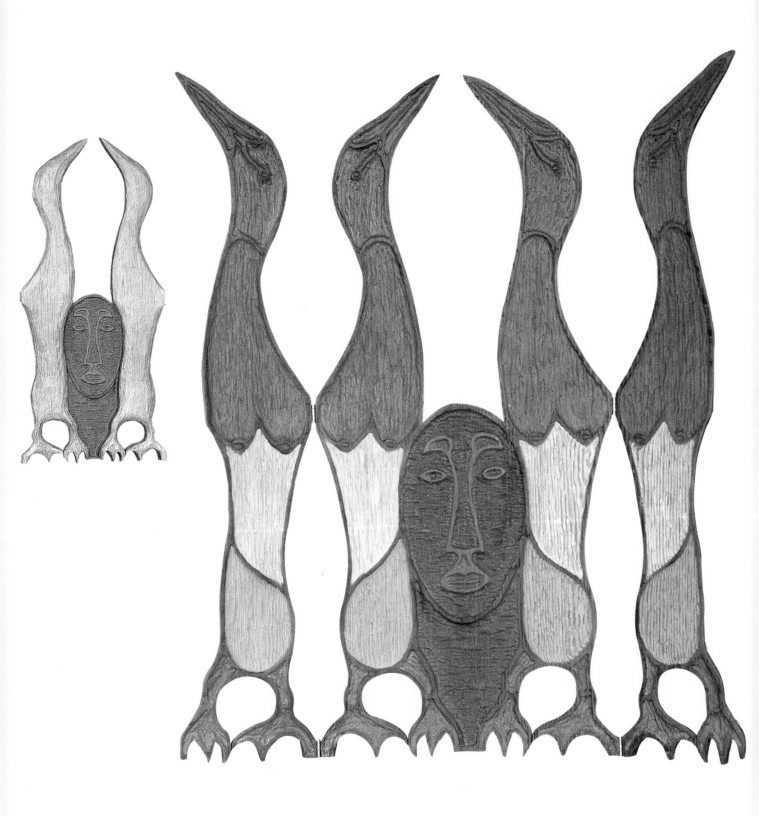

Plate 87
Blue-Footed Boobies, 1998
Cedar, 27 x 12 in. (closed);
27 x 22 in. (open)

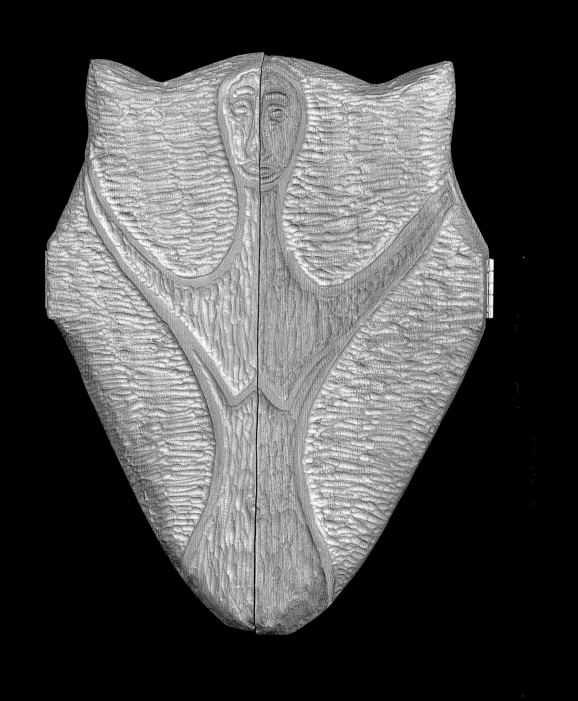

Plate 88
She Wolf, 1998
Cedar. 16 x 12 in. (closed)
16 x 24 in. (open)

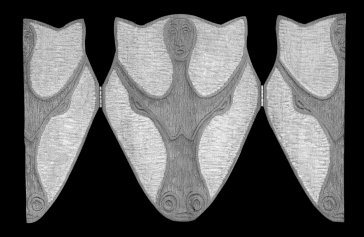

PLATE 89
Salmon Man, 1999
Cedar, 19 x 19 in.

Plate 90
Salmon Woman, 1999
Cedar, 24 x 24 in.

PLATE 91
Puffin Sunrise, 1999
Cedar, 36 x 48 in.

PLATE 92
Heronisian Moon Goddess, 1995
Cedar, 36 x 60 in.

PLATE 93
Aleut Star Dancer, 1999
Cedar, 48 x 36 in.

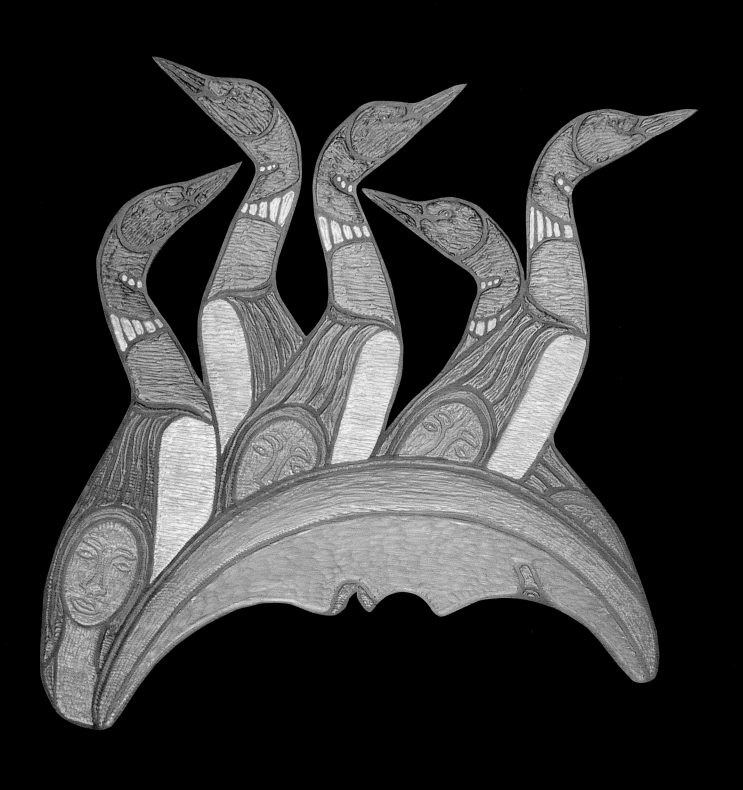

PLATE 94
Looner Eclipse, 1999
Cedar, 40 x 48 in.

Plate 95
Sensuous, 2000
Cedar, 21 x 11 in.

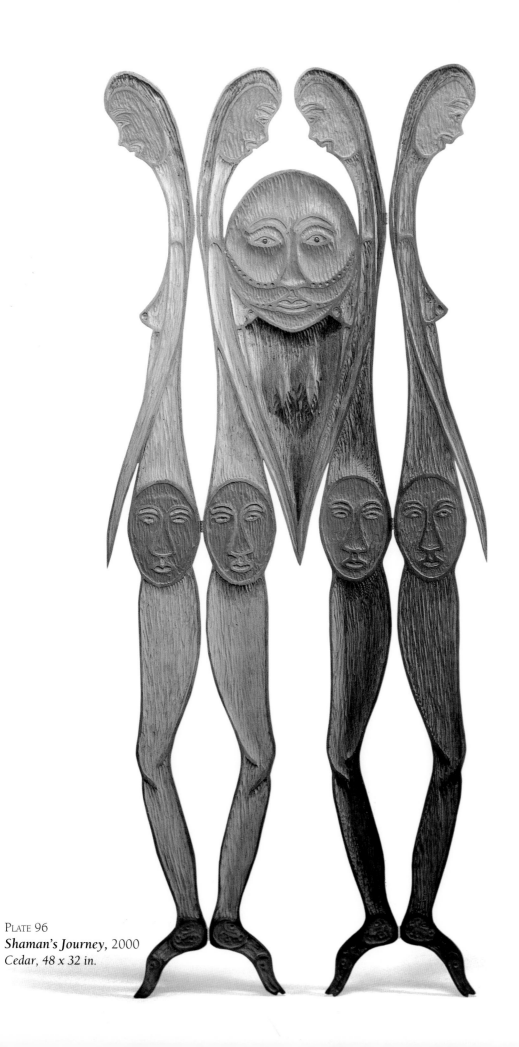

PLATE 96
Shaman's Journey, 2000
Cedar, 48 x 32 in.

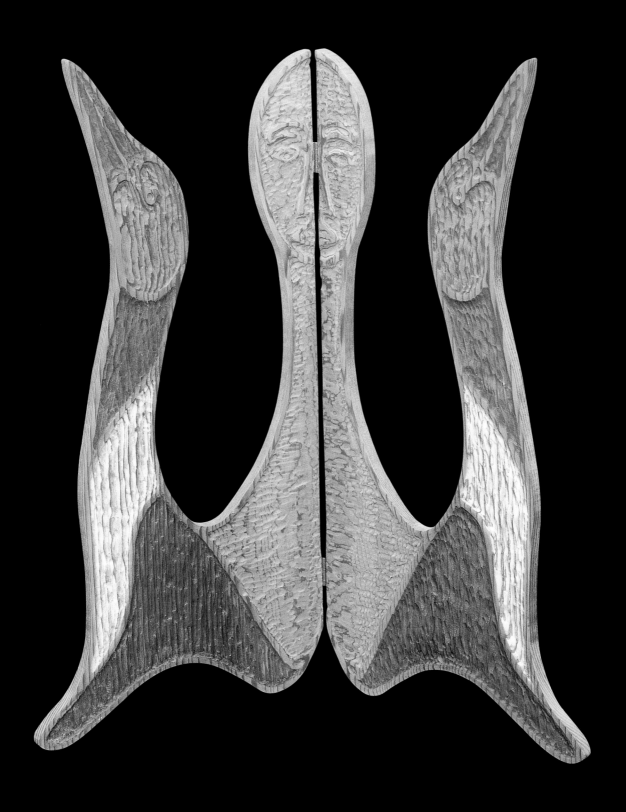

PLATE 97
Loon Woman, 2000
Cedar, 23 x 22 in.

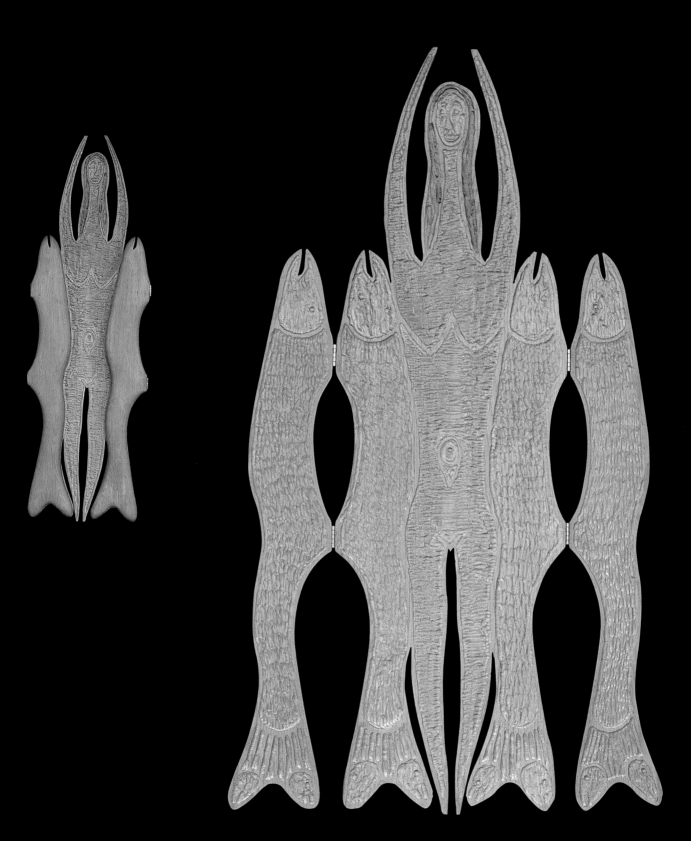

Plate 98
Salmon Woman, 2000
Cedar, 36 x 11 in. (closed)
6 x 20 in. (open)

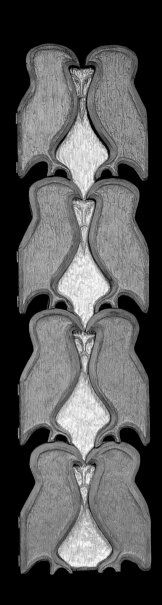

PLATE 99
Russian Priest Totem, 2000
Cedar, 48 x 12 in. (closed)
48 x 24 in. (open)

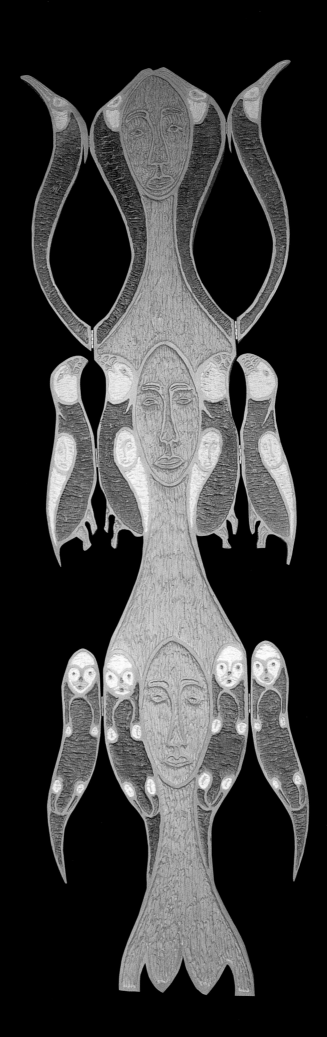

PLATE 100
Aleut Totem, 2000
Cedar, 76 x 12 in. (closed)
76 x 23 in. (open)

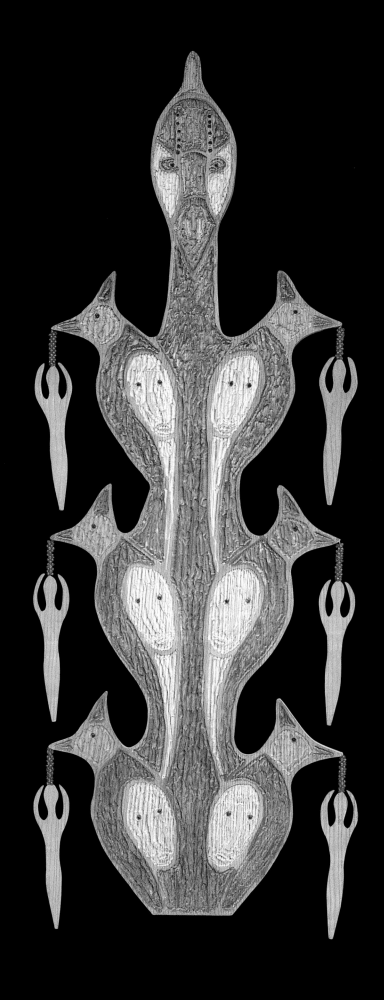

PLATE 101
Blue Jay Totem, 2000
Cedar, 49 x 17 in.

PLATE 102
Beachmaster, 2000
Cedar, 50 x 28 in.

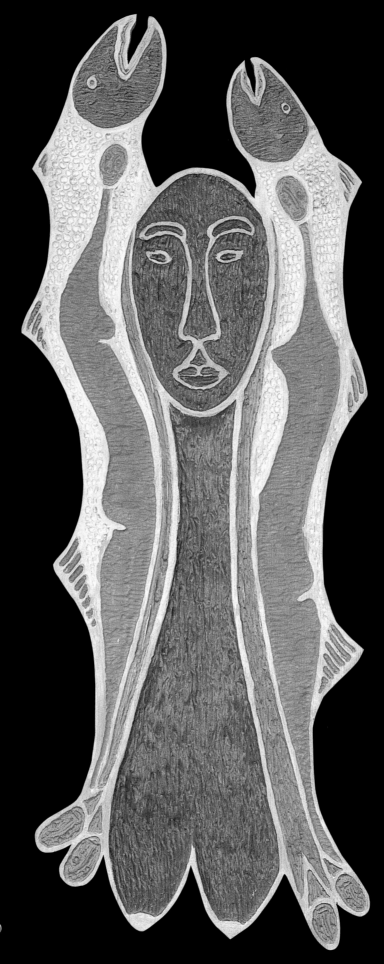

PLATE 103
Salmon Woman, 2000
Cedar, 39 x 15 in.

PLATE 104
Homage to the Otter, 2000
Cedar, 53 x 53 in.

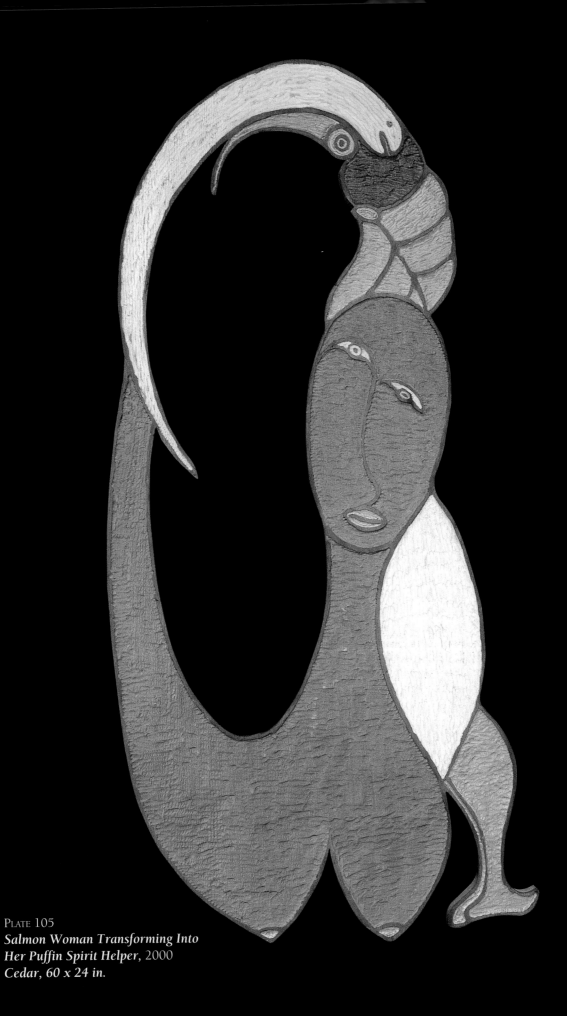

PLATE 105
**Salmon Woman Transforming Into
Her Puffin Spirit Helper**, 2000
Cedar, 60 x 24 in.

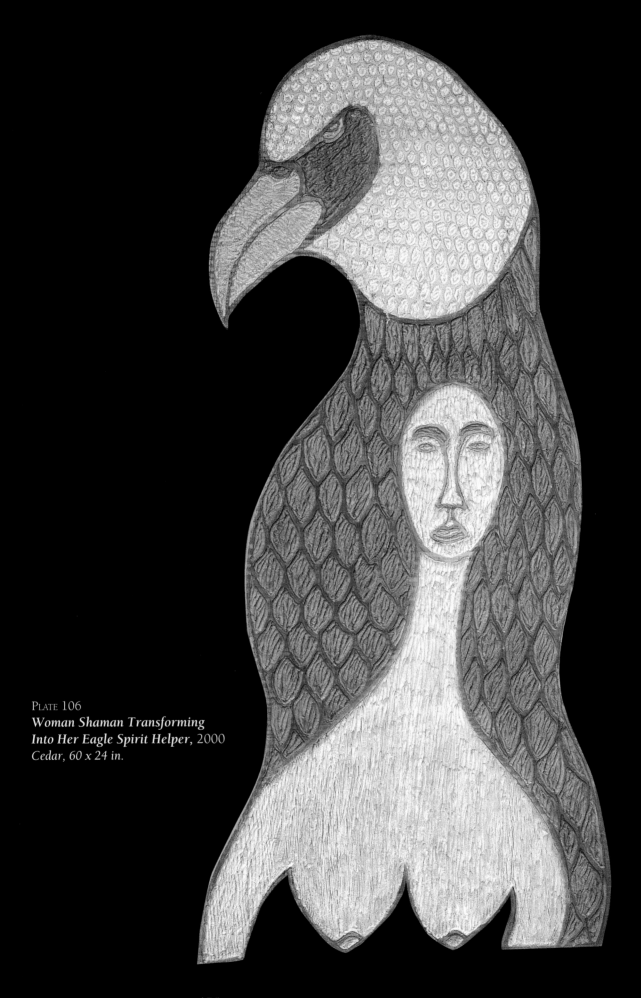

Plate 106
**Woman Shaman Transforming
Into Her Eagle Spirit Helper,** 2000
Cedar, 60 x 24 in.

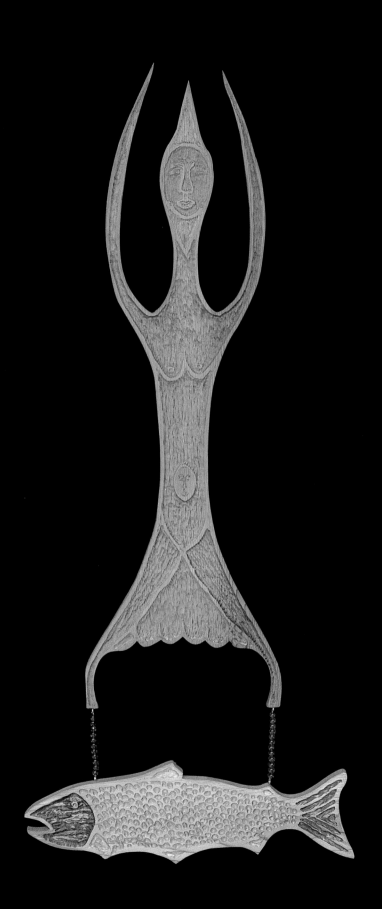

Plate 107
Salmon Woman, 2000
Cedar, 36 x 16 in.

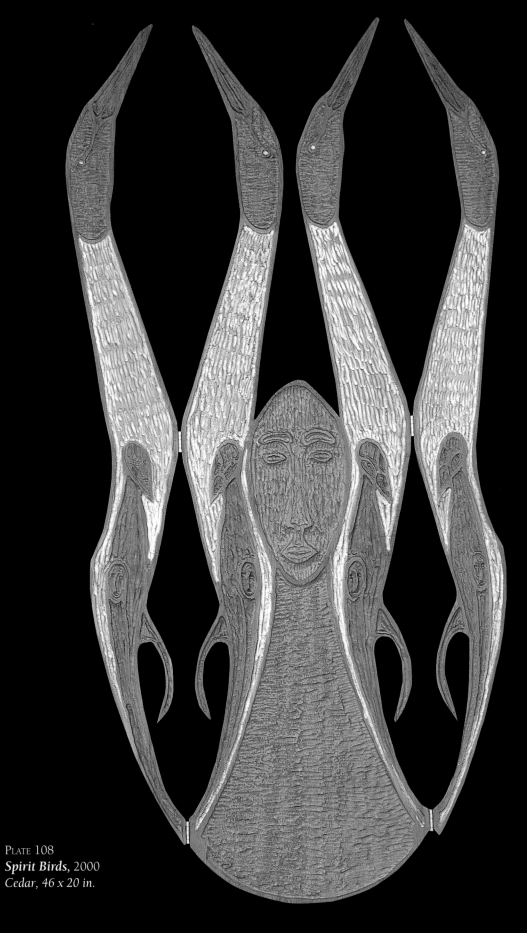

PLATE 108
Spirit Birds, 2000
Cedar, 46 x 20 in.

SELECTED PUBLIC & CORPORATE COLLECTIONS

Alaska Native Medical Center, U.S. Department of Public Health, Anchorage, Alaska

Alaska State Museum, Juneau, Alaska

Allan Houser Museum, Santa Fe, New Mexico

Anchorage Museum of History and Art, Anchorage, Alaska

Bureau of Indian Affairs, U.S. Department of the Interior, Washington, D.C.

Chugiak High School, Chugiak, Alaska

Daybreak Star Center, Seattle, Washington

Doyon Corporation, Fairbanks, Alaska

Gulf States Paper Company, Tuscaloosa, Alabama

Heard Museum, Phoenix, Arizona

Institute of American Indian Arts Museum, Santa Fe, New Mexico

King County Arts Commission, Washington

King County Courthouse, Seattle, Washington

L.A. County Museum of Natural History, Los Angeles, California

Mears Junior High School, Anchorage, Alaska

Municipality of Anchorage, Alaska

Philbrook Museum of Art, Tulsa, Oklahoma

Seattle Arts Commission, Washington

Seattle Art Museum, Washington

Sheldon Memorial Art Gallery, Lincoln, Nebraska

Tyonek Corporation, Anchorage, Alaska

Unalaska City School, Alaska

University of Alaska Museum, Fairbanks, Alaska

William A. Egan Civic and Convention Center, Anchorage, Alaska

SELECTED BIBLIOGRAPHY

Books

Ames, Kenneth M., and Herbert D.G. Mascher. *People of the Northwest Coast: Their Archaeology and Prehistory.* London: Thames & Hudson, 1999.

Archuleta, Margaret. *Twentieth Century American Sculpture at The White House: Honoring Native America.* Phoenix, Arizona: The Heard Museum of Anthropology and Primitive Art, 1997.

Black, Lydia T. *Aleut Art.* Anchorage: Aang Angain Press, Aleutian / Pribilof Islands Association, 1982.

Decker, Julie. *Icebreakers: Alaska's Most Innovative Artists.* Anchorage: Decker Art Services, 1999.

Dixon-Kennedy. *Native American Myth and Legend.* London: Blanford,1996.

Fitzhugh, William W., and Aron Crowell. *Crossroads of Continents: Cultures of Siberia and Alaska.* Washington, D.C.: Smithsonian Institution Press, 1988.

Highwater, Jamake. *The Sweetgrass Lives On.* New York: Lippencott & Crowell, 1980.

Hoffman, Gerhard, and Christian F. Feest, *Indianische Kunst im 20. Jahrhundert.* Munich: Prestel-Verlag, 1985.

Holm, Bill. *Northwest Coast Indian Art: An Analysis of Form.* Seattle: University of Washington Press, 1965.

Houllian, Patrick T. *Invitational Sculpture.* Phoenix, Arizona: The Heard Museum of Anthropology and Primitive Art, 1977.

Johnson, Maggie. *John Hoover.* Alaska Artists Solo Exhibition Series Catalogue. Anchorage: Anchorage Museum of History and Art, 1990.

Katz, Jane B. *This Song Remembers: Self-Portraits of Native Americans in the Arts.* Boston: Houghton Mifflin, 1980.

Ray, Dorothy Jean. *Aleut and Eskimo Art.* Seattle: University of Washington Press, 1980.

Ritter, Harry. *Alaska's History: The People, the Land and Events of the North Country.* Anchorage: Alaska Northwest Books, 1993.

Shearar, Cheryl. *Understanding Northwest Coast Art: A Guide to Crests, Beings and Symbols.* Seattle: University of Washington Press, 2000.

Stewart, Hilary. *Cedar.* Seattle: University of Washington Press, 1984.

Wade, Edwin L. *The Arts of the North American Indian: Native Traditions in Evolution.* New York and Tulsa, Oklahoma: Hudson Hills Press, in association with Philbrook Museum of Art, 1986.

Articles, Essays, Interviews & Periodicals

Ament, Deloris Tarzan. "Artists' Works Full of Nature's Power." *The Seattle Times,* 24 February 1993: C2.

Anstine, Dennis. Totem Tidings: "The Sculptor is a Fisherman or the Fisherman is a Sculptor." *The Daily Olympian Sunday,* 24 Oct, 1976.

Banks, Kenneth. "Visage Transcended: Contemporary Native American Masks." *Native Vision: a Bimonthly Arts Newsletter Published by American Indian Contemporary Arts.* Vol II. No 5, Nov-Dec 1985.

Bedard, Paul. "Hillary Fetes American Indian Sculptors: Art Displayed in White House Garden." *The Washington Times,* 6 Nov 1977: A11.

Decker, Julie. 1998 Artist questionnaire for *Icebreakers: Alaska's Most Innovative Artists.* Anchorage: Decker Art Services, 1999.

———. Personal recorded interview with John Hoover, January, 2000.

Dunham, Mike. "Linked by Heritage: Two Artists With Roots in Alaska Find Fame in What Makes Them Different." *Anchorage Daily News*, 27 November 1994: K1.

Dunham, Mike. "Art After Alaska: Expatriate Artists...{New lives on Puget Sound} ." *Anchorage Daily News*, 13 September 1998, K1.

Elek, Cynthia. "'Sporting Art' Displays Understated, Unified Theme." *The Anchorage Times*, 14 April 1985: K3.

Fair, Susan W. 1985. *Alaska Geographic: Alaska Native Arts and Crafts.* Vol. 12, No. 3.

Hackett, Regina. "Artist Calls on the Spirits With His Cedar Sculptures." *The Seattle Post-Intelligencer*, 12 September 1982: D5.

___. "Riches from the Bering Strait and Alaska Buried in Gallery." *The Seattle Post-Intelligencer*, 16 February 1996: 18.

Ingram, Jan. "Egan Center Sculptures Relief from Typical Art Projects." *Anchorage Daily News*, 14 October 1984: H3.

———. "Animal Life the Only Unifying Element in Exhibition." *Anchorage Daily News*, 14 April 1985: E3.

Lohrengel, Mike. "Grapeview Man Creates Art From Cedar." *The Daily Olympian*, 5 April 1973.

Metzger, Jeanne. "John, Barbara Hoover Exhibit Sculpture, Paintings at Haines." *Everett Herald-Western Sun,* 25 October 1975.

Miller, Marlan. "Week Offers Wide Variety of New Shows." *The Phoenix Gazette*, 20 October 1973.

Monathan, Doris and Guy Monathan. "John Hoover." *American Indian Art Magazine,* Winter 1978.

Myers, Patricia. "Native American Art Talks Are Scheduled." *Arizona Republic and Gazette,* 29 March 1996.

Niatum, Duane. Transcribed personal interview with John Hoover, 1996.

———. "Shamanism, Sacred Narratives, the Sea, and Cedar in the Art of John Hoover, Aleut Sculptor." University of Michigan Ph.D. dissertation (0127), 1997.

Nielsen, Nicki J. "Yesterday Along the Copper Trail. *Alaska Geographic*, Volume 15, no. 4, 1989.

Peterson, Gary. "Artisans of the Arctic." *The Anchorage Times*, 19 March 1987: C1.

Raether, Keith. "Native American Art Defined: Show Highlights N.M. Works." *Albuquerque Tribune*, 5 April 1986.

Stabler, David. "Public Comes Face to Face With Sculpture." *Anchorage Daily News*, 27 May 1984: E1.

Spatz, Ronald. "Alaska Native Writers, Storytellers and Orators." *Alaska Quarterly Review*. Anchorage: University of Alaska, 1999.

Tsutakawa, Mayumi. "Pryor Buys Sculpture, Gives It Back to Daybreak Star Center." *The Seattle Times*, 12 Dec 1979.

Ulrich, Linda. "'Blue Heron' Art Given to Sheldon to Honor Anderson." *Journal Star*, 17 April 1983. Lincoln, Nebraska.

Updike, Robin. "A Rich Mix of Ethnic Arts and Crafts Will Be On Exhibit at the Folklife Festival." *The Seattle Times,* 26 May 1994: E1.

Vasikof, Martha. Personal interview by Julie Decker. Anchorage, Alaska, November 6, 2000.

———. "Africa, Alaska Folklife Focus." *The Olympian*, 27 May 1994.

———. *The Bellingham Review*, Twentieth Issue (Fall). Edited by Randy Jay Landon and Knute Skinner. Signpost Press, Inc.

———. "Indian Art on Show at Museum." *The Daily Olympian*, 15 October 1976.

————. *Jeopardy*, Volume 21: Spring 1985. Western Washington University.

————. *Journal of Alaska Native Arts*, March-April 1988. Alaska State Council on the Arts.

————. *Journal of Alaska Native Arts*, Jan-Feb-Mar 1993. Alaska State Council on the Arts.

————. "Myths Flavor Grapeview Artist's Work." *Shelton-Mason County Journal*, 6 September 1984.

————. "New Artwork Added to Convention Center." *Guide to Events at the Sullivan Arena and Egan Center*, Summer 1984.

————. "Sculptor's Work Greets Public at Egan Convention Center." *Anchorage Daily News*, 27 May 1984.

PHOTOGRAPHY AND REPRODUCTION CREDITS

Figures

Unless otherwise specified, figure illustrations are personal photographs provided by the artist.

Photographs Courtesy of the Anchorage Museum of History and Art: Figures 5, 6, 11, 37
Volcano Woman is installed at the William A. Egan Convention Center through the public art
   program of the Municipality of Anchorage. This artwork is part of the collection of the
   Anchorage Museum of History and Art.
Photographs by Mary Randlett: Figures 18–21, 23–26, 28, 33, 35, 36
Photographs by Steve Cox: Figures 27, 29–32, 38, 44

Plates

All works illustrated as plates are from the collection of John and Mary Hoover or held by
   collectors who prefer to remain anonymous, except:

Plate 36
Shaman's Tree of Life, 1985
Collection of the Anchorage Museum of History and Art

Plate 42
Salmon Women, 1985
Collection of Mike and Joanne Hoskins

Plate 76
Otter People, 1995
Collection of Jim O. Llewellyn

Plate 88
She Wolf, 1998
Collection of Anna Hoover

Photographs by Steve Cox: Plates 1–17, 21–24, 32–37, 40, 44–53, 56, 60–62, 67, 74–77,
   79, 80, 82, 83, 85-88, 93–108
Photographs by Mary Randlett: Plates 18–20, 25–31
Photographs by Steve Vento: Plates 38–43, 55–59, 63, 65, 66, 70, 71, 73, 81
Photograph by Hart W. Empie: Plate 54
Photograph by Chris Arend Photography: Plate 64
Photographs by James H. Barker: Plates 68, 69, 72, 78, 84, 89–92

John Hoover: Art & Life
was produced for the University of Washington Press
by Perpetua Press, Santa Barbara

Edited by Letitia O'Connor and Kathy Talley-Jones
Designed by Dana Levy
Printed in Hong Kong by Toppan Printing Co.

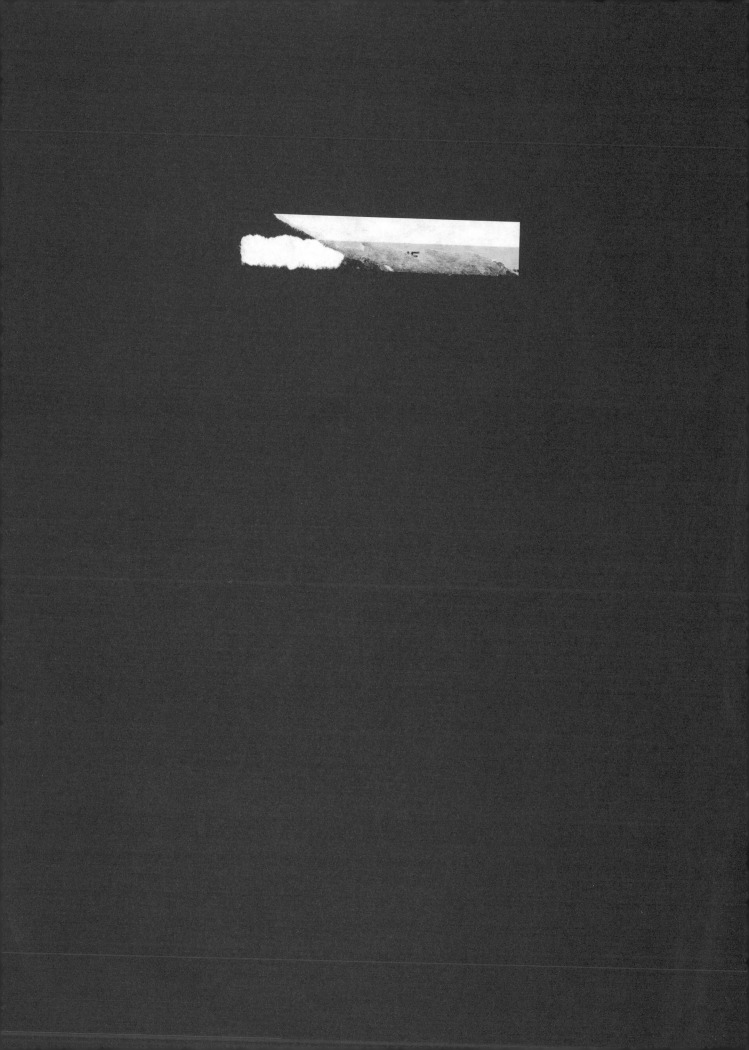